HOW MARKETS REALLY WORK

Since 1996, Bloomberg Press has published books for financial professionals on investing, economics, and policy affecting investors. Titles are written by leading practitioners and authorities, and have been translated into more than 20 languages.

The Bloomberg Financial Series provides both core reference knowledge and actionable information for financial professionals. The books are written by experts familiar with the work flows, challenges, and demands of investment professionals who trade the markets, manage money, and analyze investments in their capacity of growing and protecting wealth, hedging risk, and generating revenue.

For a list of available titles, please visit our website at www.wiley.com/go/bloombergpress.

HOW MARKETS REALLY WORK

A Quantitative Guide to Stock Market Behavior

Second Edition

Laurence A. Connors
Cesar Alvarez
Connors Research LLC

BLOOMBERG PRESS
An Imprint of
WILEY

Published by John Wiley & Sons, Inc., Hoboken, New Jersey.
Published simultaneously in Canada.

First edition published by The Connors Group in 2004.

For general information on our other products and services or for technical support, please contact our Customer Care Department within the United States at (800) 762-2974, outside the United States at (317) 572-3993 or fax (317) 572-4002.

Wiley also publishes its books in a variety of electronic formats. Some content that appears in print may not be available in electronic books. For more information about Wiley products, visit our website at www.wiley.com.

Library of Congress Cataloging-in-Publication Data:

Connors, Laurence A.
    How markets really work : a quantitative guide to stock market behavior / Laurence A. Connors, Cesar Alvarez. — Second edition.
        1 online resource. — (Bloomberg financial series ; 158)
    Includes index.
    Description based on print version record and CIP data provided by publisher; resource not viewed.
    ISBN 978-1-118-16650-5 (cloth); ISBN 978-1-118-22628-5 (ebk);
    ISBN 978-1-118-23945-2 (ebk); ISBN 978-1-118-26420-1 (ebk);
        1. Stock exchanges—United States.   I. Alvarez, Cesar, 1967–   II. Title.
HG4910
332.64'2—dc23
                                                                                                2011050882

Printed in the United States of America

10 9 8 7 6 5 4 3 2 1

Contents

CHAPTER 10

CHAPTER 11

CHAPTER 12

CHAPTER 13

CHAPTER 14

Disclaimer

It should not be assumed that the methods, techniques, or indicators presented in this book will be profitable or that they will not result in losses. Past results are not necessarily indicative of future results. Examples in this book are for educational purposes only. The author, publishing firm, and any affiliates assume no responsibility for your trading results. This is not a solicitation of any order to buy or sell.

HYPOTHETICAL OR SIMULATED PERFORMANCE RESULTS HAVE CERTAIN INHERENT LIMITATIONS. UNLIKE AN ACTUAL PERFORMANCE RECORD, SIMULATED RESULTS DO NOT REPRESENT ACTUAL TRADING. ALSO, SINCE THE TRADES HAVE NOT ACTUALLY BEEN EXECUTED, THE RESULTS MAY HAVE UNDER- OR OVERCOMPENSATED FOR THE IMPACT, IF ANY, OF CERTAIN MARKET FACTORS, SUCH AS LACK OF LIQUIDITY. SIMULATED TRADING PROGRAMS IN GENERAL ARE ALSO SUBJECT TO THE FACT THAT THEY ARE DESIGNED WITH THE BENEFIT OF HINDSIGHT. NO REPRESENTATION IS BEING MADE THAT ANY ACCOUNT WILL OR IS LIKELY TO ACHIEVE PROFITS OR LOSSES SIMILAR TO THOSE SHOWN.

Table Explanation

Following is an explanation of each of the columns in the tables that appear at the end of Chapters 2 through 11.

1. The "Index" column indicates which market we tested, either the S&P 500 (SPX) or the Nasdaq 100 (NDX).
2. "Rule 1" describes the first rule of the test. We would take a position only if this condition occurred.
3. "Rule 2" is the second rule of the test, if applicable. If this column contains information, then both rule 1 and rule 2 must be in place to take a position. If this column is blank, then only rule 1 is needed.
4. The "Time Period" column indicates the length of a single test. "1 day" means buy today, sell tomorrow. "1 week" means buy today, exit five trading days from now.
5. The "Gain/Loss" column lists the average percentage gain or loss the market made while we were in the position with the specified rules.
6. The "# Winners" column tallies up the number of profitable tests for the given set of rules.
7. The "# Days" column tallies up the number of times that our set of rules produced a trade.
8. The "% Profitable" column is simply the number of winners divided by the total number of trades.
9. In every test we wanted to have a baseline for comparison. We called this our "Benchmark Average." The benchmark average is the average percentage the market gained or lost during the specified time period overall length of the test interval. For instance, the average one-day gain of the S&P 500 from January 1989 to September 2011 was 0.03%.
10. The "% Profitable Benchmark" column serves as a profitability comparison between our trade signal and the typical market. It takes all market periods and calculates what percentage of them were profitable.

Acknowledgments

Special thank you to David Weilmuenster, Leigh Lommen, and Danilo Torres for their assistance in helping us with this book.

CHAPTER 1

Market Edges

The following is verbatim from the first edition of How Markets Really Work. *It's important to get a point of reference of what we wrote and saw in 2004 compared to what we see with the second edition, which was written in late 2011.*

■ ■ ■

For many of us, Michael Lewis's 1989 best-selling book *Liar's Poker* was the first inside look at what day-to-day life was like at a major Wall Street trading firm. Lewis described in detail, the wheeling and dealing of some of the famous (and infamous) Wall Street titans who oversaw billions of dollars of transactions every trading day during the 1980s. The book remains a classic today but 14 years after it was published, Lewis outdid himself. In 2003, he published *Moneyball: The Art of Winning an Unfair Game*. The book chronicles the success of the Oakland A's, who under the guidance of their general manager, Billy Beane, used massive amounts of statistical data to help them successfully run their ball team.

The A's essentially turned their backs on the old school of thinking, much of which was intuitive, and attempted to turn baseball into a science. Players who should have been fifteenth-round draft picks were being chosen by the A's near the top of the draft (and signed very cheaply). These types of players were chosen not because they looked good or the scouting reports said they couldn't miss. They were chosen because the statistics said that these players had an edge and that this edge had a better chance of playing itself out than the guessing that had gone into past selections. Essentially, Billy Beane and the A's turned baseball upside down, and by relying upon numbers instead of opinion, they have been able to successfully compete against teams that had far more money to spend on talent.

The godfather behind this move to relying upon numbers instead of gut is a brilliant gentleman by the name of Bill James. In the 1970s James began publishing studies and then books on player evaluation and baseball strategy. Up until a few years ago, James was all but ignored by mainstream baseball. Hall of Fame manager

Sparky Anderson, who is the only manager to win a World Series in both the National League and the American League, referred to James as "a fat guy with a beard who knows nothing about nothing." And in spite of the success that the A's and a few other teams have had relying upon statistics, the debate still rages as to its effectiveness. But, as this is being written, baseball has begun the process of turning away from the Sparky Anderson school of knowledge and accepting the thinking of people like Bill James. General managers are being hired by teams not for their baseball playing careers or their baseball prowess, but for their ability to analyze baseball statistics and make correct decisions using these statistics. Teams like the Red Sox and the Dodgers now have GMs who are only in their early thirties. Why are they entrusted with franchises that are valued in the hundreds of millions of dollars? It's because these guys don't guess. *They know numbers and their understanding of these numbers provides them with an edge.*

And in some cases, this edge is substantial.

What does this have to do with trading? A lot. After we read *Moneyball,* we remarked that it's amazing that baseball has gone this route yet most of Wall Street still has not. If baseball has quantified mainstream parts of the game such as batting average, on base percentage, errors, steals, walks, and so on, why hasn't Wall Street done the same with the indicators it relies upon every day? Trading day after trading day, we are bombarded with information from the media. "The market rose for the third straight day as the bulls are taking charge." What does this mean? It sounds good, doesn't it? It sure feels as though the market is going to continue to rise. A market rising three days in a row is usually rising because of good news. Isn't that a precursor of things to come? What about advancing issues and declining issues? On days when the market drops sharply and declining stocks far outnumber advancing stocks, the press and the analysts tell us this is bad. Poor market breadth is supposedly a sign of future weakness. It seems to make sense. But is it true? (You'll soon see it's not.)

Just as old school baseball used to think that a guy who was 6′3″ and could run fast and hit the ball a mile was a can't-miss prospect, much of old-school Wall Street still thinks that good news and market strength is a sign of future upward price movement and bad news and poor market strength is a sign of future downward movement. As you will soon learn, at least looking at the market over the past 15 years (1989–2003), there is nothing further from the truth. This is not our opinion or guess. *It's what the statistics show.* And just as baseball had a tough time accepting the fact that on-base percentage is more important than batting average, we suspect that many people on Wall Street, especially the media and the mainstream firms, will have a tough time accepting the fact that *it's better over the near term for the market to have dropped than for it to have risen.*

All combined, we have nearly three decades of trading and research experience behind us. Much of what you will learn from this book is a culmination of our work. We looked at a number of the most common ways traders, analysts, and the press look at the market. Even though we went into the tests having a strong clue where the results would end up, even we were surprised at some of these results. The tests included us looking at how the S&P 500 cash market (SPX) and the Nasdaq 100 cash market (NDX) did over a 1-day, 2-day, and 1-week period after they made a 5-period high, 10-period high, 5-period low, and 10-period low (intraday). We also looked at how these markets did after prices rose multiple days in a row (showing strength) and declined multiple days in a row (showing weakness). We looked at the times when the markets made multiple-day higher highs and multiple-day lower lows, again looking at what happened after continuous strength and weakness. From there we looked at the days when the market rose sharply to the upside versus declined sharply to the downside.

Volume was another topic we tackled, as it is one of the most often-used indicators. After volume, you'll learn about market breadth when we analyze what the market has done after advancing issues outperformed declining issues (and vice versa). The results from many of these chapters may surprise you, and this chapter may be the biggest surprise.

From there, we looked at another common indicator: new 52-week highs and new 52-week lows. There's a healthy edge here, and again it's not where the analysts and the press say it is. In the final two chapters, we'll show you how to use the put/call ratio and the volatility index (VIX)—Chicago Board Options Exchange (CBOE) Volatility Index. Each indicator has shown strong consistent edges, and we'll teach you where these edges are.

Before we move to the next chapter and start looking at the test results, we'd like to cover a few guidelines to help you better understand how to use this book and how to use the information presented to help gain a greater edge in your trading and investing.

1. We'll state this again later in the book, but you need to know that there are no assurances that these test results will hold up in the future. Even though many of these tests are independent of one another and basically lead to the same conclusion, it cannot be assumed this conclusion (or any market conclusion) will hold true in the future.
2. Much of Wall Street is made up of opinions. It's also made up of opinions that are not backed by any statistical evidence. If the baseball world can do it, then Wall Street can do it, too. Hopefully, this book is just the tip of the iceberg in using statistics to help understand how markets behave and how one can make proper and rational decisions on a day-to-day basis.
3. All these tests were run on the cash market and were not actual trades. Also, commissions and slippage were not factored in.
4. *All the tests use a benchmark.* This means we compared apples to apples. We looked at the results when certain situations occurred versus how the market performed on average during the same time period. We did the same for the percentage of trades that showed gains. In many cases we could have shown more test results, but we didn't because the number of opportunities that occurred (the sample size) was too low.
5. We tested the S&P 500 and the Nasdaq 100 cash markets throughout the book.
6. Many of the tests run as far back as 15 years. This encompassed a solid bull market, followed by a very severe bear market, followed by a rally in 2003. The net bias

was up for the entire time frame, but the market also saw some healthy selling periods, especially from 2000 to 2002.

7. Finding clean market data is not as easy as one would think. There are data vendors whose data we could not trust. Therefore, we used data from sources we trusted, including the CBOE for the put/call ratio tests and the VIX tests. In many cases we tested up to 15 years of data, but in some cases we had to use fewer years in order not to compromise the integrity of the test results. These tests were run multiple times in order to assure the results. If you elect to do your own testing and find different results, it might possibly be due to the data your data vendor is providing.

8. In many chapters we also looked at the market trend. We defined the market trend as being up when the market was above its 200-day moving average (200-day ma) and down when it was below its 200-day moving average.

9. None of these tests are systems, nor should they be traded as systems, nor do we trade them alone as systems. They simply look at how markets behaved over a fixed period of time in specific market conditions.

10. This book can be used by everyone and should provide you with a basic philosophy for looking at the markets. Traders especially will be able to use this information as the focus of the book is on the short-term. But interestingly enough, you will see the same type of statistical evidence in long-term investing using the basic philosophy and concepts from this book at www.TheMachineAdvisor.com (the site is related to us).

11. Please understand that the results you will see are average returns. This means that there were gains and losses in any individual scenario that were far from average. And going forward, there will undoubtedly be situations that occur that will be far from the averages published here.

12. You'll see one common theme throughout this book: *Buying short-term weakness has outperformed buying short-term strength over the past 15 years.* Should this trend continue, there is a big edge here for traders to take advantage of. The goal of this work is to show you when these times occurred and what the historical edge has been.

■ ■ ■

What Has Changed Since We Originally Wrote This

It's nearly eight years later, and in spite of a market that has since risen significantly, dropped significantly (crashed), and then risen again, *much of what we saw back then still holds true today.*

Even the baseball analogy discussing how teams that rely upon data outperform teams that don't rely upon data has continued to prove true. The Red Sox have since won two World Series (2004 and 2007) and the St. Louis Cardinals have also won twice (2006 and 2011).

Data used properly—whether in baseball or in the markets—still works.

In this updated edition, we took the tests we originally published and updated them through the third quarter of 2011 (we wrote this book as soon as the quarter ended and submitted it to our publisher in November 2011). What you will see is that markets have continued to work the way they worked from 1989 to 2003. There is now up to 22¾ years of data here, and the overriding theme is that *on a short-term basis, oversold markets tend to move higher over the next few days and overbought markets tend to move lower on a short-term basis over the next few days.*

This behavior doesn't mean it happens every time. As in baseball performance, market performance is a game of averages. Identify where the averages have had edges, and then look to exploit those edges over and over again. That's the main focus of the book.

We've also added three new chapters to the book. The first chapter (Chapter 11) relies upon an oscillator, which we have published research on for many years, and we believe may be the best oscillator to identify overbought and oversold market conditions (the numbers support this statement).

We also added a chapter on long-term market behavior (one year) that shows conclusively that low volatility stocks outperform high volatility stocks (Chapter 12). Not only do they outperform, they do so with far less risk. This chapter will be of special interest to anyone who manages a longer-term portfolio of stocks.

We wrapped up the additional research by building a short-term strategy with the concepts in this book, which only trades in S&P 500 stocks (Chapter 13). This simple strategy has outperformed the S&P 500 index by over 10 percent a year in simulated trading and did so with 70 percent lower volatility. On a cumulative basis the return has been well over 100 percent since 2001 and shows that one can potentially do quite well investing in mostly blue chip stocks by following a few simple rules that apply the concepts from this book.

People like to say markets change. We disagree. Technology changes, *but market behavior rarely does*, especially short-term. Markets are made up of individuals, and individuals are driven by the same emotions no matter what decade or even century they're in. Yes, intelligence has greatly expanded but decisions are still driven by fear and greed, especially at market extremes no matter what the time frame. *Our goal is to quantify these emotions, and in this book you will see that over the past two plus decades, in spite of the incredible technology, product and global expansion in the markets, they still behave the same way over and over again.*

We hope you enjoy this second edition of *How Markets Really Work*. Now, let's move on to the updated research.

CHAPTER 2

Short-Term Highs and Short-Term Lows

Many traders and investors have been taught to buy strength and sell weakness. Buying new short-term highs is supposed to be the sign of a healthy market, and selling new short-term lows is supposed to be the sign of a weak market. Our results over a more than 22-year period show the exact opposite.

The highlights of the results include the fact that buying new 10-day highs in the S&P 500 (SPX) lost money when exiting one week later. In a powerful bull market, you would have actually lost money by buying these new highs and exiting a week later. Said another way, *for the past two decades, prices on average have been lower, not higher, one week after the market has made a short-term new high.*

Let's now look at a few of our test results.

The Market Has Declined (on Average) Following 5- and 10-Day Highs

1. First we looked at the S&P 500 from January 1, 1989, through September 30, 2011. We then looked at how the SPX performed every day during that period of time. We found that the SPX had gained an average of 0.03 percent per day and an average of 0.15 percent per week for the 22+-year period, reflecting the bull market move.

   We then looked at the average daily gain of the SPX after it made a new 5-day (intraday) high. Remember, new highs are supposedly a sign of strength, are breakouts, and are considered by many a time to buy.

   What we found was the opposite. These new highs underperformed the average daily market. Their average daily gain for the next day was 0.00 percent. We also looked at how these breakouts did over the next week, and again we saw them performing poorly. *In fact, the average 1-week gain was –0.02 percent, far less than the average weekly gain of 0.15 percent over the same time period.*

Ten-day new highs, which are considered even stronger markets to be buying, showed even worse results. Their average daily gain after the SPX made a new 10-day high was –0.02 percent. The weekly results were just as poor, showing an average return of –0.03 percent.

Returns Increased Following 5- and 10-Day Losses

2. We then looked at when markets were acting poorly. We looked at the performance of the SPX after it made a new 5-day low.

Again, our findings were completely at odds with conventional wisdom. We found that the average daily gain after a 5-day low was 0.07 percent. The average weekly gain was 0.43 percent, outperforming the average week and far outperforming the week following a new 5-day high. The 10-day new lows showed similar performance. The average daily gain following a 10-day new low was 0.13 percent and 0.51 percent for the weekly gain.

New Highs Made under the 200-Day Moving Average Strongly Underperformed

3. We also looked at the impact that trend had with a market making a new short-term high versus a new short-term low. We found that, buying a new 5-day high when the SPX was trading under its 200-day moving average showed a 1-day return of –0.12 percent and only a one-week loss of –0.25 percent. Ten-day new highs lost money both the next day (–0.14 percent) and the next week (–0.35 percent). These results show that bear traps do exist when markets rally while trading under their 200-day moving average, and you would probably be wise to avoid buying equities during these days.

Pullbacks within the Direction of the Trend Are Significant: Rallies Counter to the Trend Underperformed

4. When you combine both price movement with trend, you see additional significant results. For example, when a 10-day low occurred in the S&P 500, when it was above its 200-day moving average, it led to higher prices 60.08 percent of the time the next day. When the index made a 10-day high below the 200-day moving average, prices rose only 46.79 percent of the time the next day.

■ ■ ■

Now let's look at the bar graphs, time charts, and the entire test results of how the SPX and the Nasdaq 100 index (NDX) have performed after making 5-day highs, 10-day highs, 5-day lows, and 10-day lows. (See Figures 2.1–2.4.)

See *Table Explanation* at the beginning of this book for column descriptions.

FIGURE 2.1 S&P 500: 5-Day Lows in the S&P 500 Significantly Outperformed 5-Day Highs

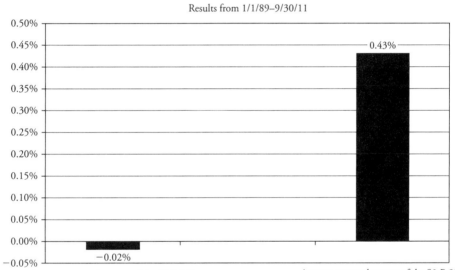

Results from 1/1/89–9/30/11

FIGURE 2.2   S&P 500: 10-Day Lows in the S&P 500 Greatly Outperformed 10-Day Highs

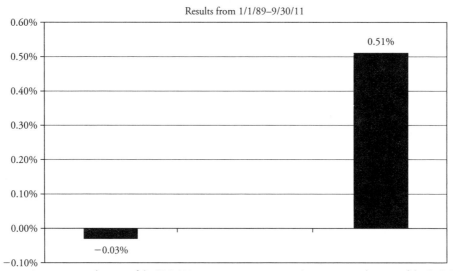

Results from 1/1/89–9/30/11

Average one-week return of the S&P 500
after the S&P 500 makes a 10-day high

Average one-week return of the S&P 500
after the S&P 500 makes a 10-day low

FIGURE 2.3 Nasdaq 100: New 5-Day Highs in the Nasdaq Underperformed versus 5-Day Lows

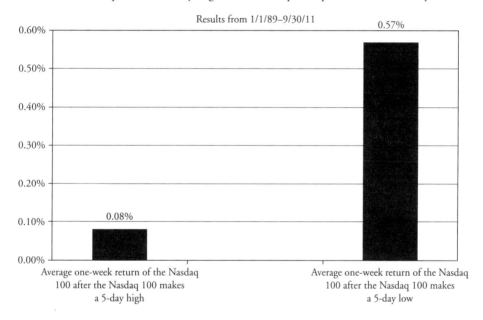

FIGURE 2.4 Nasdaq 100: 10-Day Lows Outperformed 10-Day Highs by a Better than 3-1 Margin

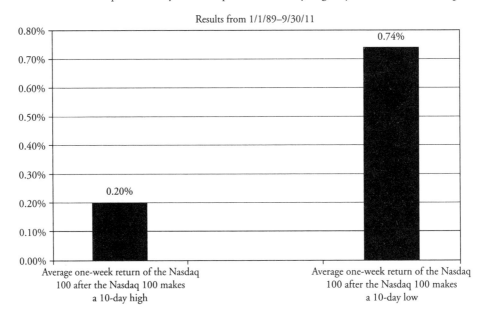

Results from 1/1/89–9/30/11

Timeline Graph Performance Explanation

These lines show the cumulative profit (or loss) in dollars that would result over time from executing a trade of 1 share for a particular index for every occurrence of the situation described. (These are often called points of profit or loss.)

For example, Figure 2.5 shows the cumulative S&P 500 points that a trader would gain/lose by buying 1 share of the S&P 500 index every time that it made a new 5-day low (or 5-day high) and then selling the position one week later. (See Figures 2.5–2.8 and Tables 2.1 and 2.2.)

See *Table Explanation* at the beginning of this book for column descriptions.

FIGURE 2.5   Time Graph Performance Comparison: S&P 500 Index Buying 5-Day Highs versus 5-Day Lows

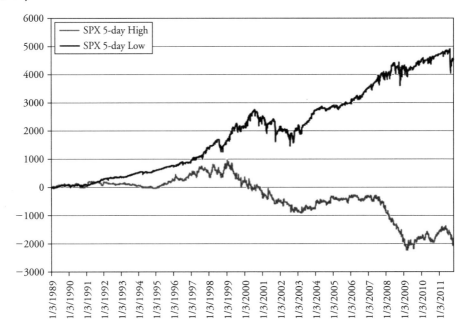

FIGURE 2.6 Time Graph Performance Comparison: S&P 500 Index Buying 10-Day Highs versus 10-Day Lows

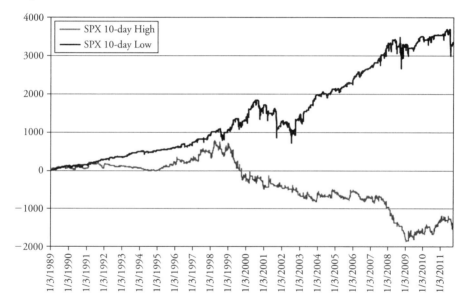

FIGURE 2.7 Time Graph Performance Comparison: Nasdaq 100 Index Buying 5-Day Highs versus 5-Day Lows

FIGURE 2.8 Time Graph Performance Comparison: Nasdaq 100 Index Buying 10-Day Highs versus 10-Day Lows

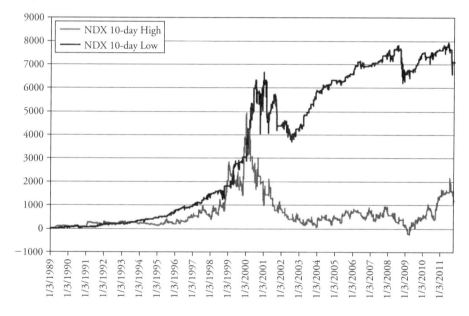

TABLE 2.1 SPX Short-Term Highs and Lows (1/1/1989 to 9/30/2011)

Index	Rule 1	Rule 2	Time Period	Gain/Loss	# Winners	# Days	% Profitable	Benchmark Average	% Profitable Benchmark
SP500	5-day high		1 day	0	1008	1955	51.56	0.03	53.43
SP500	5-day high		2 days	−0.02	1006	1955	51.46	0.06	53.92
SP500	5-day high		1 week	−0.02	1052	1955	53.81	0.15	56.19
SP500	10-day high		1 day	−0.02	721	1441	50.03	0.03	53.43
SP500	10-day high		2 days	−0.07	722	1441	50.1	0.06	53.92
SP500	10-day high		1 week	−0.03	769	1441	53.37	0.15	56.19
SP500	21-day high		1 day	−0.01	564	1110	50.81	0.03	53.43
SP500	21-day high		2 days	−0.03	558	1110	50.27	0.06	53.92
SP500	21-day high		1 week	−0.02	591	1110	53.24	0.15	56.19
SP500	5-day low		1 day	0.07	755	1385	54.51	0.03	53.43
SP500	5-day low		2 days	0.15	767	1385	55.38	0.06	53.92
SP500	5-day low		1 week	0.43	825	1385	59.57	0.15	56.19
SP500	10-day low		1 day	0.13	494	873	56.59	0.03	53.43
SP500	10-day low		2 days	0.22	499	873	57.16	0.06	53.92
SP500	10-day low		1 week	0.51	517	873	59.22	0.15	56.19
SP500	21-day low		1 day	0.11	298	538	55.39	0.03	53.43
SP500	21-day low		2 days	0.19	298	538	55.39	0.06	53.92
SP500	21-day low		1 week	0.46	305	538	56.69	0.15	56.19
SP500	5-day high	Above 200-day MA	1 day	0.02	822	1573	52.26	0.04	54.12
SP500	5-day high	Above 200-day MA	2 days	0.01	826	1573	52.51	0.08	55.29
SP500	5-day high	Above 200-day MA	1 week	0.03	862	1573	54.8	0.19	57.22
SP500	10-day high	Above 200-day MA	1 day	0	619	1223	50.61	0.04	54.12

SP500	10-day high	Above 200-day MA	2 days	−0.03	625	1223	51.1	0.08	55.29
SP500	10-day high	Above 200-day MA	1 week	0.02	661	1223	54.05	0.19	57.22
SP500	21-day high	Above 200-day MA	1 day	0.01	503	984	51.12	0.04	54.12
SP500	21-day high	Above 200-day MA	2 days	−0.01	502	984	51.02	0.08	55.29
SP500	21-day high	Above 200-day MA	1 week	0.04	533	984	54.17	0.19	57.22
SP500	5-day low	Above 200-day MA	1 day	0.06	473	840	56.31	0.04	54.12
SP500	5-day low	Above 200-day MA	2 days	0.15	478	840	56.9	0.08	55.29
SP500	5-day low	Above 200-day MA	1 week	0.45	522	840	62.14	0.19	57.22
SP500	10-day low	Above 200-day MA	1 day	0.11	286	476	60.08	0.04	54.12
SP500	10-day low	Above 200-day MA	2 days	0.24	283	476	59.45	0.08	55.29
SP500	10-day low	Above 200-day MA	1 week	0.59	303	476	63.66	0.19	57.22
SP500	21-day low	Above 200-day MA	1 day	0.09	137	231	59.31	0.04	54.12
SP500	21-day low	Above 200-day MA	2 days	0.18	132	231	57.14	0.08	55.29
SP500	21-day low	Above 200-day MA	1 week	0.48	140	231	60.61	0.19	57.22
SP500	5-day high	Below 200-day MA	1 day	−0.12	186	382	48.69	0.01	51.7
SP500	5-day high	Below 200-day MA	2 days	−0.16	180	382	47.12	0.02	50.52
SP500	5-day high	Below 200-day MA	1 week	−0.25	190	382	49.74	0.06	53.6
SP500	10-day high	Below 200-day MA	1 day	−0.14	102	218	46.79	0.01	51.7
SP500	10-day high	Below 200-day MA	2 days	−0.28	97	218	44.5	0.02	50.52
SP500	10-day high	Below 200-day MA	1 week	−0.35	108	218	49.54	0.06	53.6
SP500	21-day high	Below 200-day MA	1 day	−0.09	61	126	48.41	0.01	51.7
SP500	21-day high	Below 200-day MA	2 days	−0.13	56	126	44.44	0.02	50.52
SP500	21-day high	Below 200-day MA	1 week	−0.51	58	126	46.03	0.06	53.6
SP500	5-day low	Below 200-day MA	1 day	0.08	282	545	51.74	0.01	51.7

(continued)

TABLE 2.1 (Continued)

Index	Rule 1	Rule 2	Time Period	Gain/Loss	# Winners	# Days	% Profitable	Benchmark Average	% Profitable Benchmark
SP500	5-day low	Below 200-day MA	2 days	0.16	289	545	53.03	0.02	50.52
SP500	5-day low	Below 200-day MA	1 week	0.41	303	545	55.6	0.06	53.6
SP500	10-day low	Below 200-day MA	1 day	0.14	208	397	52.39	0.01	51.7
SP500	10-day low	Below 200-day MA	2 days	0.2	216	397	54.41	0.02	50.52
SP500	10-day low	Below 200-day MA	1 week	0.43	214	397	53.9	0.06	53.6
SP500	21-day low	Below 200-day MA	1 day	0.13	161	307	52.44	0.01	51.7
SP500	21-day low	Below 200-day MA	2 days	0.19	166	307	54.07	0.02	50.52
SP500	21-day low	Below 200-day MA	1 week	0.45	165	307	53.75	0.06	53.6

TABLE 2.2 NDX Short-Term Highs and Lows (1/1/1989 to 9/30/2011)

Index	Rule 1	Rule 2	Time Period	Gain/Loss	# Winners	# Days	% Profitable	Benchmark Average	% Profitable Benchmark
NDX100	5-day high		1 day	0.05	1084	1972	54.97	0.06	54.26
NDX100	5-day high		2 days	0.06	1049	1972	53.19	0.12	53.54
NDX100	5-day high		1 week	0.08	1076	1972	54.56	0.29	56.17
NDX100	10-day high		1 day	0.05	815	1469	55.48	0.06	54.26
NDX100	10-day high		2 days	0.06	784	1469	53.37	0.12	53.54
NDX100	10-day high		1 week	0.2	814	1469	55.41	0.29	56.17
NDX100	21-day high		1 day	0.04	616	1099	56.05	0.06	54.26
NDX100	21-day high		2 days	0.08	599	1099	54.5	0.12	53.54
NDX100	21-day high		1 week	0.18	622	1099	56.6	0.29	56.17
NDX100	5-day low		1 day	0.13	798	1448	55.11	0.06	54.26
NDX100	5-day low		2 days	0.23	787	1447	54.39	0.12	53.54
NDX100	5-day low		1 week	0.57	831	1447	57.43	0.29	56.17
NDX100	10-day low		1 day	0.26	496	893	55.54	0.06	54.26
NDX100	10-day low		2 days	0.35	498	893	55.77	0.12	53.54
NDX100	10-day low		1 week	0.74	527	893	59.01	0.29	56.17
NDX100	21-day low		1 day	0.26	295	545	54.13	0.06	54.26
NDX100	21-day low		2 days	0.32	293	545	53.76	0.12	53.54
NDX100	21-day low		1 week	0.64	316	545	57.98	0.29	56.17
NDX100	5-day high	Above 200-day MA	1 day	0.08	884	1592	55.53	0.07	54.97
NDX100	5-day high	Above 200-day MA	2 days	0.14	862	1592	54.15	0.14	54.62
NDX100	5-day high	Above 200-day MA	1 week	0.22	894	1592	56.16	0.36	57.34

(continued)

TABLE 2.2 (*Continued*)

Index	Rule 1	Rule 2	Time Period	Gain/Loss	# Winners	# Days	% Profitable	Benchmark Average	% Profitable Benchmark
NDX100	10-day high	Above 200-day MA	1 day	0.07	700	1247	56.13	0.07	54.97
NDX100	10-day high	Above 200-day MA	2 days	0.11	679	1247	54.45	0.14	54.62
NDX100	10-day high	Above 200-day MA	1 week	0.27	708	1247	56.78	0.36	57.34
NDX100	21-day high	Above 200-day MA	1 day	0.06	551	971	56.75	0.07	54.97
NDX100	21-day high	Above 200-day MA	2 days	0.13	536	971	55.2	0.14	54.62
NDX100	21-day high	Above 200-day MA	1 week	0.25	560	971	57.67	0.36	57.34
NDX100	5-day low	Above 200-day MA	1 day	0.09	483	858	56.29	0.07	54.97
NDX100	5-day low	Above 200-day MA	2 days	0.25	488	858	56.88	0.14	54.62
NDX100	5-day low	Above 200-day MA	1 week	0.7	511	858	59.56	0.36	57.34
NDX100	10-day low	Above 200-day MA	1 day	0.2	265	459	57.73	0.07	54.97
NDX100	10-day low	Above 200-day MA	2 days	0.43	275	459	59.91	0.14	54.62
NDX100	10-day low	Above 200-day MA	1 week	1	296	459	64.49	0.36	57.34
NDX100	21-day low	Above 200-day MA	1 day	0.1	120	208	57.69	0.07	54.97
NDX100	21-day low	Above 200-day MA	2 days	0.28	121	208	58.17	0.14	54.62
NDX100	21-day low	Above 200-day MA	1 week	0.63	122	208	58.65	0.36	57.34
NDX100	5-day high	Below 200-day MA	1 day	−0.07	200	380	52.63	0.04	52.52
NDX100	5-day high	Below 200-day MA	2 days	−0.25	187	380	49.21	0.06	50.85
NDX100	5-day high	Below 200-day MA	1 week	−0.5	182	380	47.89	0.14	53.26
NDX100	10-day high	Below 200-day MA	1 day	−0.09	115	222	51.8	0.04	52.52
NDX100	10-day high	Below 200-day MA	2 days	−0.22	105	222	47.3	0.06	50.85
NDX100	10-day high	Below 200-day MA	1 week	−0.19	106	222	47.75	0.14	53.26
NDX100	21-day high	Below 200-day MA	1 day	−0.17	65	128	50.78	0.04	52.52

NDX100	21-day high	Below 200-day MA	2 days	−0.29	63	128	49.22	0.06	50.85
NDX100	21-day high	Below 200-day MA	1 week	−0.38	62	128	48.44	0.14	53.26
NDX100	5-day low	Below 200-day MA	1 day	0.18	315	590	53.39	0.04	52.52
NDX100	5-day low	Below 200-day MA	2 days	0.21	299	589	50.76	0.06	50.85
NDX100	5-day low	Below 200-day MA	1 week	0.39	320	589	54.33	0.14	53.26
NDX100	10-day low	Below 200-day MA	1 day	0.32	231	434	53.23	0.04	52.52
NDX100	10-day low	Below 200-day MA	2 days	0.27	223	434	51.38	0.06	50.85
NDX100	10-day low	Below 200-day MA	1 week	0.46	231	434	53.23	0.14	53.26
NDX100	21-day low	Below 200-day MA	1 day	0.35	175	337	51.93	0.04	52.52
NDX100	21-day low	Below 200-day MA	2 days	0.35	172	337	51.04	0.06	50.85
NDX100	21-day low	Below 200-day MA	1 week	0.65	194	337	57.57	0.14	53.26

Summary and Conclusion

As you can see, the greater opportunity and edge lies in being a buyer as the market makes a new short-term low versus buying when it makes a new high.

Why is this so? It's because a market usually makes a new high after good news has occurred. This good news could be economic reports, earnings, and more. The buying has already occurred. On the opposite side, new lows are usually accompanied by bad economic news, bad earnings, and so on. The sellers have taken prices lower, and from there the buyers get to step in, especially those correctly anticipating better news in the near future.

In conclusion, the statistics show that it has been better to be a buyer of new short-term lows, rather than a buyer of new short-term highs (breakouts).

Now let's look at the times when the market has made multiple days of higher highs and multiple days of lower lows.

CHAPTER 3

Higher Highs
and Lower Lows

The questions we asked here were, "Is it better to be a buyer after the market has been strong and has made multiple days of higher highs? And is it better to be a seller after the market has shown signs of weakness and has made multiple days of lower lows?"

It is generally accepted that markets that make multiple higher highs in a row are strong and markets that make multiple lower lows in a row are weak. A higher high simply means that today's intraday high (not close) was higher than yesterday's intraday high. A lower low means that today's intraday low was lower than yesterday's intraday low.

In this chapter, we look at the times when the S&P 500 (SPX) and the Nasdaq 100 (NDX) (separately) made three or more days of consecutive higher highs. During these times the market is behaving strongly. Yesterday's high was above the previous day's high and today's high is even higher. We also look at the times when the SPX and the NDX made three or more consecutive lower lows. These are usually selling days, and these selling days are supposedly a sign of future weakness.

We looked at the market over a 22+-year period (January 1989–September 2011), and a summary of our findings is as follows.

The Market Lost Money within One Week after Three or More Consecutive Days of Higher Highs

1. After the market made three or more higher highs, it underperformed the averages the next week. In fact, the S&P 500 has lost money (net) within a week after making a three-or-more-day higher high (again, in spite of an upward market bias).

Multiple Days of Lower Lows Outperformed the Average Daily Gain

2. The opposite is true for lows. Weakness, as defined by the market making multiple day lows, is followed on average by strength. Three, four, and five days in a row lows outperform the average day after one day, two days, and one week.

25

Multiple-Day Lows Far Outperformed Multiple-Day Highs

3. This is most significant: When we matched up what the market did after making multiple higher highs versus making multiple lower lows, we see significant edges. For example, when the market makes five lower lows in a row, the average weekly gain has been 0.39 percent. When it has made five higher highs in a row, the market on average has lost –0.09 percent over the next week.

Multiple-Day Lows in the Nasdaq Outperformed Multiple-Day Highs

4. The same types of results are seen when looking at the Nasdaq 100. Multiple-day lows outperform multiple-day highs by a wide per trade margin.

See *Table Explanation* at the beginning of this book for column descriptions.

FIGURE 3.1 S&P 500 Three Consecutive Days Higher Highs in the S&P 500 Has Led on Average to Negative Returns after One Week

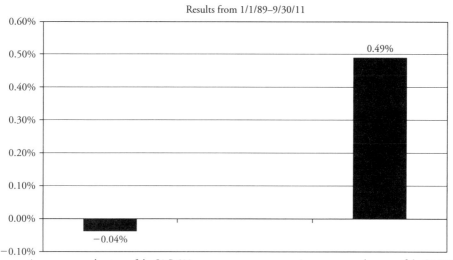

Results from 1/1/89–9/30/11

FIGURE 3.2   S&P 500 Four Consecutive Days of Lower Lows Has Led to Returns Far Greater than Four Consecutive Days of Higher Highs

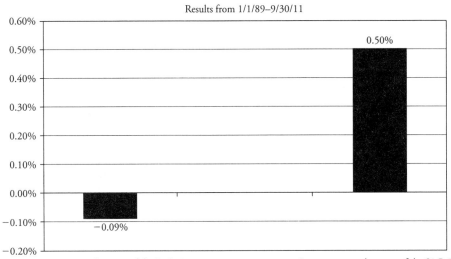

Results from 1/1/89–9/30/11

FIGURE 3.3 Nasdaq 100: Three Consecutive Days of Lower Lows in the Nasdaq Has Led (on Average) to Greater Returns than Three Consecutive Higher Highs after One Week

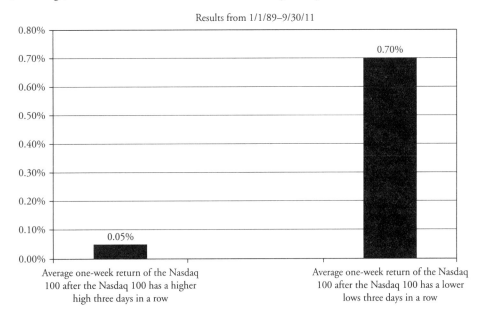

Results from 1/1/89–9/30/11

FIGURE 3.4 Nasdaq 100: Four Consecutive Days of Lower Lows in the Nasdaq Has Led (on Average) to Significantly Greater Returns than Four Consecutive Days of Higher Highs after One Week

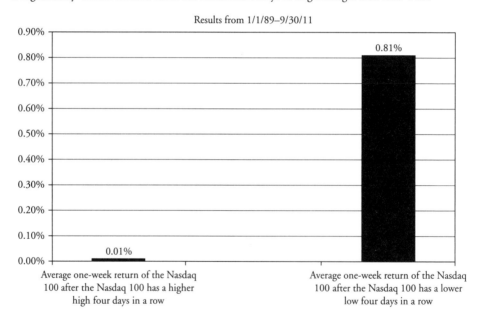

FIGURE 3.5 Time Graph Performance Comparison: S&P 500 Index Buying Higher High Three Days in a Row versus Buying a Lower Low Three Days in a Row

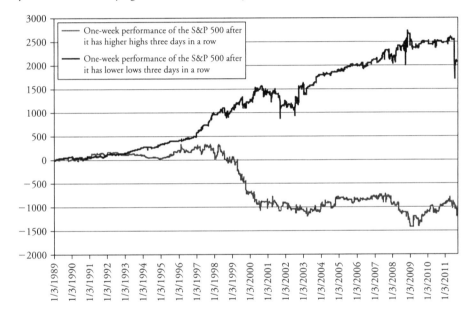

FIGURE 3.6 Time Graph Performance Comparison: S&P 500 Index Results from Buying a Higher High Four Days in a Row versus Buying a Lower Low Four Days in a Row

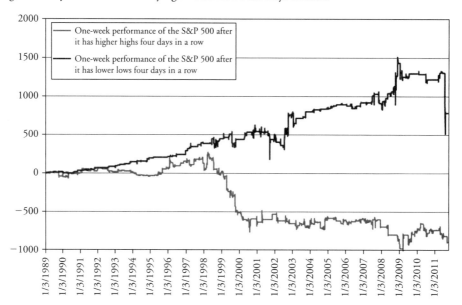

FIGURE 3.7 Time Graph Performance Comparison: Nasdaq 100 Index Buying a Higher High Three Days in a Row versus Buying a Lower Low Three Days in a Row

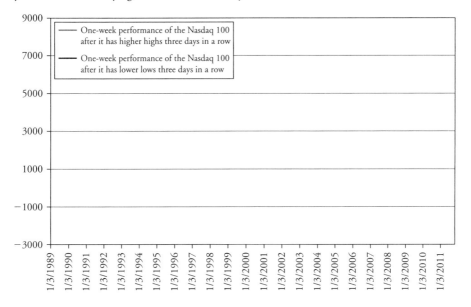

FIGURE 3.8   Time Graph Performance Comparison: Nasdaq 100 Index Buying a Higher High Four
Days in a Row versus Buying a Lower Low Four Days in a Row

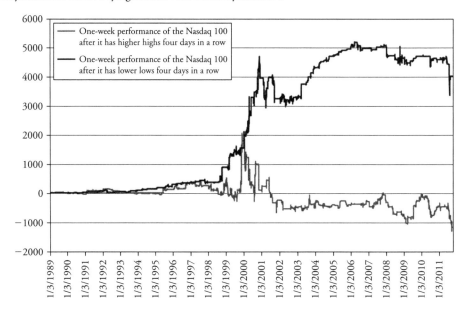

TABLE 3.1 SPX Higher Highs and Lower Lows (1/1/1989 to 9/30/2011)

Index	Rule 1	Rule 2	Time Period	Gain/Loss	# Winners	# Days	% Profitable	Benchmark Average	% Profitable Benchmark
SP500	Higher high 3 days in a row		1 day	0.02	498	968	51.45	0.03	53.43
SP500	Higher high 3 days in a row		2 days	0.02	523	968	54.03	0.06	53.92
SP500	Higher high 3 days in a row		1 week	−0.04	528	968	54.55	0.15	56.19
SP500	Higher high 4 days in a row		1 day	0.02	283	541	52.31	0.03	53.43
SP500	Higher high 4 days in a row		2 days	0.02	291	541	53.79	0.06	53.92
SP500	Higher high 4 days in a row		1 week	−0.09	283	541	52.31	0.15	56.19
SP500	Higher high 5 days in a row		1 day	0.04	152	306	49.67	0.03	53.43
SP500	Higher high 5 days in a row		2 days	0.05	155	306	50.65	0.06	53.92
SP500	Higher high 5 days in a row		1 week	−0.09	158	306	51.63	0.15	56.19
SP500	Lower low 3 days in a row		1 day	0.18	359	626	57.35	0.03	53.43
SP500	Lower low 3 days in a row		2 days	0.25	360	626	57.51	0.06	53.92
SP500	Lower low 3 days in a row		1 week	0.49	379	626	60.54	0.15	56.19
SP500	Lower low 4 days in a row		1 day	0.27	163	280	58.21	0.03	53.43
SP500	Lower low 4 days in a row		2 days	0.34	167	280	59.64	0.06	53.92
SP500	Lower low 4 days in a row		1 week	0.5	169	280	60.36	0.15	56.19
SP500	Lower low 5 days in a row		1 day	0.38	80	127	62.99	0.03	53.43
SP500	Lower low 5 days in a row		2 days	0.36	79	127	62.2	0.06	53.92
SP500	Lower low 5 days in a row		1 week	0.39	75	127	59.06	0.15	56.19
SP500	Higher high 3 days in a row	Above 200-day MA	1 day	0.05	420	799	52.57	0.04	54.12
SP500	Higher high 3 days in a row	Above 200-day MA	2 days	0.06	442	799	55.32	0.08	55.29
SP500	Higher high 3 days in a row	Above 200-day MA	1 week	−0.02	438	799	54.82	0.19	57.22

(*continued*)

TABLE 3.1 (*Continued*)

Index	Rule 1	Rule 2	Time Period	Gain/Loss	# Winners	# Days	% Profitable	Benchmark Average	% Profitable Benchmark
SP500	Higher high 4 days in a row	Above 200–day MA	1 day	0.04	248	468	52.99	0.04	54.12
SP500	Higher high 4 days in a row	Above 200–day MA	2 days	0.02	255	468	54.49	0.08	55.29
SP500	Higher high 4 days in a row	Above 200–day MA	1 week	−0.08	246	468	52.56	0.19	57.22
SP500	Higher high 5 days in a row	Above 200–day MA	1 day	0.04	137	273	50.18	0.04	54.12
SP500	Higher high 5 days in a row	Above 200–day MA	2 days	0.03	138	273	50.55	0.08	55.29
SP500	Higher high 5 days in a row	Above 200–day MA	1 week	−0.12	143	273	52.38	0.19	57.22
SP500	Lower low 3 days in a row	Above 200–day MA	1 day	0.17	211	351	60.11	0.04	54.12
SP500	Lower low 3 days in a row	Above 200–day MA	2 days	0.3	210	351	59.83	0.08	55.29
SP500	Lower low 3 days in a row	Above 200–day MA	1 week	0.5	230	351	65.53	0.19	57.22
SP500	Lower low 4 days in a row	Above 200–day MA	1 day	0.17	87	144	60.42	0.04	54.12
SP500	Lower low 4 days in a row	Above 200–day MA	2 days	0.25	87	144	60.42	0.08	55.29
SP500	Lower low 4 days in a row	Above 200–day MA	1 week	0.31	97	144	67.36	0.19	57.22
SP500	Lower low 5 days in a row	Above 200–day MA	1 day	0.31	38	57	66.67	0.04	54.12
SP500	Lower low 5 days in a row	Above 200–day MA	2 days	0.21	36	57	63.16	0.08	55.29
SP500	Lower low 5 days in a row	Above 200–day MA	1 week	0.13	38	57	66.67	0.19	57.22
SP500	Higher high 3 days in a row	Below 200–day MA	1 day	−0.12	78	169	46.15	0.01	51.7
SP500	Higher high 3 days in a row	Below 200–day MA	2 days	−0.14	81	169	47.93	0.02	50.52
SP500	Higher high 3 days in a row	Below 200–day MA	1 week	−0.16	90	169	53.25	0.06	53.6
SP500	Higher high 4 days in a row	Below 200–day MA	1 day	−0.14	35	73	47.95	0.01	51.7
SP500	Higher high 4 days in a row	Below 200–day MA	2 days	−0.01	36	73	49.32	0.02	50.52
SP500	Higher high 4 days in a row	Below 200–day MA	1 week	−0.15	37	73	50.68	0.06	53.6

SP500	Higher high 5 days in a row	Below 200-day MA	1 day	0.01	15	33	45.45	0.01	51.7
SP500	Higher high 5 days in a row	Below 200-day MA	2 days	0.23	17	33	51.52	0.02	50.52
SP500	Higher high 5 days in a row	Below 200-day MA	1 week	0.13	15	33	45.45	0.06	53.6
SP500	Lower low 3 days in a row	Below 200-day MA	1 day	0.19	148	275	53.82	0.01	51.7
SP500	Lower low 3 days in a row	Below 200-day MA	2 days	0.2	150	275	54.55	0.02	50.52
SP500	Lower low 3 days in a row	Below 200-day MA	1 week	0.48	149	275	54.18	0.06	53.6
SP500	Lower low 4 days in a row	Below 200-day MA	1 day	0.38	76	136	55.88	0.01	51.7
SP500	Lower low 4 days in a row	Below 200-day MA	2 days	0.44	80	136	58.82	0.02	50.52
SP500	Lower low 4 days in a row	Below 200-day MA	1 week	0.71	72	136	52.94	0.06	53.6
SP500	Lower low 5 days in a row	Below 200-day MA	1 day	0.44	42	70	60	0.01	51.7
SP500	Lower low 5 days in a row	Below 200-day MA	2 days	0.48	43	70	61.43	0.02	50.52
SP500	Lower low 5 days in a row	Below 200-day MA	1 week	0.6	37	70	52.86	0.06	53.6

TABLE 3.2 NDX Higher Highs and Lower Lows (1/1/1989 to 9/30/2011)

Index	Rule 1	Rule 2	Time Period	Gain/Loss	# Winners	# Days	% Profitable	Benchmark Average	% Profitable Benchmark
NDX100	Higher high 3 days in a row		1 day	0.07	590	1082	54.53	0.06	54.26
NDX100	Higher high 3 days in a row		2 days	0.06	580	1082	53.6	0.12	53.54
NDX100	Higher high 3 days in a row		1 week	0.05	585	1082	54.07	0.29	56.17
NDX100	Higher high 4 days in a row		1 day	−0.01	336	646	52.01	0.06	54.26
NDX100	Higher high 4 days in a row		2 days	−0.04	340	646	52.63	0.12	53.54
NDX100	Higher high 4 days in a row		1 week	0.01	346	646	53.56	0.29	56.17
NDX100	Higher high 5 days in a row		1 day	0	204	380	53.68	0.06	54.26
NDX100	Higher high 5 days in a row		2 days	−0.09	197	380	51.84	0.12	53.54
NDX100	Higher high 5 days in a row		1 week	0.16	208	380	54.74	0.29	56.17
NDX100	Lower low 3 days in a row		1 day	0.21	425	743	57.2	0.06	54.26
NDX100	Lower low 3 days in a row		2 days	0.24	402	743	54.11	0.12	53.54
NDX100	Lower low 3 days in a row		1 week	0.7	432	743	58.14	0.29	56.17
NDX100	Lower low 4 days in a row		1 day	0.31	223	386	57.77	0.06	54.26
NDX100	Lower low 4 days in a row		2 days	0.38	212	386	54.92	0.12	53.54
NDX100	Lower low 4 days in a row		1 week	0.81	223	386	57.77	0.29	56.17
NDX100	Lower low 5 days in a row		1 day	0.45	116	199	58.29	0.06	54.26
NDX100	Lower low 5 days in a row		2 days	0.49	114	199	57.29	0.12	53.54
NDX100	Lower low 5 days in a row		1 week	0.84	110	199	55.28	0.29	56.17
NDX100	Higher high 3 days in a row	Above 200-day MA	1 day	0.07	496	900	55.11	0.07	54.97
NDX100	Higher high 3 days in a row	Above 200-day MA	2 days	0.09	491	900	54.56	0.14	54.62
NDX100	Higher high 3 days in a row	Above 200-day MA	1 week	0.14	498	900	55.33	0.36	57.34

NDX100	Higher high 4 days in a row	Above 200-day MA	1 day	0.02	292	554	52.71	0.07	54.97
NDX100	Higher high 4 days in a row	Above 200-day MA	2 days	0.04	303	554	54.69	0.14	54.62
NDX100	Higher high 4 days in a row	Above 200-day MA	1 week	0.16	308	554	55.6	0.36	57.34
NDX100	Higher high 5 days in a row	Above 200-day MA	1 day	0.05	187	338	55.33	0.07	54.97
NDX100	Higher high 5 days in a row	Above 200-day MA	2 days	0.03	185	338	54.73	0.14	54.62
NDX100	Higher high 5 days in a row	Above 200-day MA	1 week	0.31	193	338	57.1	0.36	57.34
NDX100	Lower low 3 days in a row	Above 200-day MA	1 day	0.21	242	403	60.05	0.07	54.97
NDX100	Lower low 3 days in a row	Above 200-day MA	2 days	0.35	232	403	57.57	0.14	54.62
NDX100	Lower low 3 days in a row	Above 200-day MA	1 week	0.79	246	403	61.04	0.36	57.34
NDX100	Lower low 4 days in a row	Above 200-day MA	1 day	0.31	113	185	61.08	0.07	54.97
NDX100	Lower low 4 days in a row	Above 200-day MA	2 days	0.46	110	185	59.46	0.14	54.62
NDX100	Lower low 4 days in a row	Above 200-day MA	1 week	0.86	114	185	61.62	0.36	57.34
NDX100	Lower low 5 days in a row	Above 200-day MA	1 day	0.49	56	87	64.37	0.07	54.97
NDX100	Lower low 5 days in a row	Above 200-day MA	2 days	0.61	55	87	63.22	0.14	54.62
NDX100	Lower low 5 days in a row	Above 200-day MA	1 week	0.8	51	87	58.62	0.36	57.34
NDX100	Higher high 3 days in a row	Below 200-day MA	1 day	0.05	94	182	51.65	0.04	52.52
NDX100	Higher high 3 days in a row	Below 200-day MA	2 days	−0.09	89	182	48.9	0.06	50.85
NDX100	Higher high 3 days in a row	Below 200-day MA	1 week	−0.37	87	182	47.8	0.14	53.26
NDX100	Higher high 4 days in a row	Below 200-day MA	1 day	−0.21	44	92	47.83	0.04	52.52
NDX100	Higher high 4 days in a row	Below 200-day MA	2 days	−0.57	37	92	40.22	0.06	50.85
NDX100	Higher high 4 days in a row	Below 200-day MA	1 week	−0.9	38	92	41.3	0.14	53.26
NDX100	Higher high 5 days in a row	Below 200-day MA	1 day	−0.38	17	42	40.48	0.04	52.52
NDX100	Higher high 5 days in a row	Below 200-day MA	2 days	−1.11	12	42	28.57	0.06	50.85
NDX100	Higher high 5 days in a row	Below 200-day MA	1 week	−1.07	15	42	35.71	0.14	53.26

(continued)

TABLE 3.2 (*Continued*)

Index	Rule 1	Rule 2	Time Period	Gain/Loss	# Winners	# Days	% Profitable	Benchmark Average	% Profitable Benchmark
NDX100	Lower low 3 days in a row	Below 200-day MA	1 day	0.22	183	340	53.82	0.04	52.52
NDX100	Lower low 3 days in a row	Below 200-day MA	2 days	0.11	170	340	50	0.06	50.85
NDX100	Lower low 3 days in a row	Below 200-day MA	1 week	0.6	186	340	54.71	0.14	53.26
NDX100	Lower low 4 days in a row	Below 200-day MA	1 day	0.3	110	201	54.73	0.04	52.52
NDX100	Lower low 4 days in a row	Below 200-day MA	2 days	0.31	102	201	50.75	0.06	50.85
NDX100	Lower low 4 days in a row	Below 200-day MA	1 week	0.76	109	201	54.23	0.14	53.26
NDX100	Lower low 5 days in a row	Below 200-day MA	1 day	0.41	60	112	53.57	0.04	52.52
NDX100	Lower low 5 days in a row	Below 200-day MA	2 days	0.39	59	112	52.68	0.06	50.85
NDX100	Lower low 5 days in a row	Below 200-day MA	1 week	0.87	59	112	52.68	0.14	53.26

Summary and Conclusion

At the beginning of this chapter we asked, "Is it better to be a buyer after the market has been strong and has made multiple days of higher highs? And is it better to be a seller after the market has shown signs of weakness and has made multiple days of lower lows?" *The answer (to both) is a resounding "no."*

As you can see, the greater opportunity and edge has been from being a buyer as the market has made lower lows versus buying when it makes higher highs. Why is this so? It is for the same reasons we discussed in the previous chapter. It's because a market usually makes a new high after good news has occurred. This good news could be a slew of positive economic reports, positive earnings, and so on. The buying has already occurred. On the opposite side, new lows are usually accompanied by bad economic news, bad earnings, and so on. The sellers have taken prices lower, and from there the buyers get to step in, especially those correctly anticipating better news in the near future.

Now let's look at when markets rise and fall consecutive days in a row.

CHAPTER 4

Up Days in a Row versus Down Days in a Row

What does the market do after it rises or falls consecutive days in a row?

Conventional wisdom states that a market that rallies a few days in a row is strong and a market that drops a few days in a row is weak. The test results prove the opposite.

Returns Increased Following Consecutive Days of Market Declines; Returns Decreased Following Consecutive Days of Market Gains

1. After the S&P 500 index (SPX) has risen three days in a row (and three days in a row); the market has underperformed the benchmark over the next one day, two days, and also over the next week. When the SPX declined two days in a row (and three days in a row), the market has proceeded to outperform the benchmark over the next one day, two days, and the next week.

Consecutive Days of Declining Markets Far Outperformed Consecutive Days of Rising Markets

2. When comparing two days up in a row to two days down in a row, the difference in the returns is significant. After the SPX has dropped two days in a row, it has risen on average 0.41 percent after one week. When it has rallied two days in a row, it has risen only 0.01 percent over the next week. The edge in three days in a row is even more significant. After the SPX has dropped three days in row the market has risen on average 0.64 percent over the next week. When it has risen three days in row, the market lost on average −0.01 percent over the following one-week period.

Nasdaq Mirrored S&P Results When Looking at Multiple Days Higher and Multiple Days Lower

3. When we look at the Nasdaq index (NDX) we see basically the same trend. Both two and three up days in a row underperform two and three down days in a row.

There is obviously an abundance of information that can be gleaned from this chapter, and we encourage you to spend time with the data.

See *Table Explanation* at the beginning of this book for column descriptions.

FIGURE 4.1 S&P 500: Down Days Have Outperformed Up Days after One Week: Said Another Way, Over the Next Week, It Was Better for the Market to Have Dropped Today

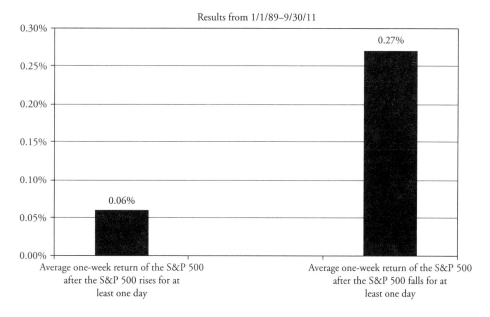

FIGURE 4.2   S&P 500: Two Down Days in a Row Outperformed Two Up Days in a Row after
One Week

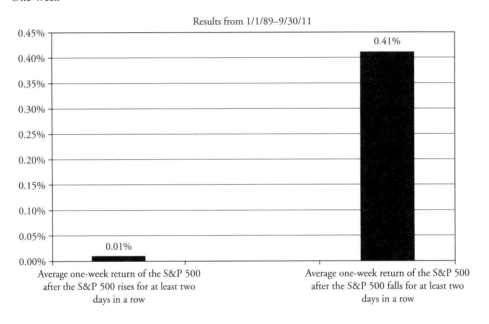

FIGURE 4.3 S&P 500: Three Down Days in a Row Vastly Outperformed Three Up Days in a Row after One Week

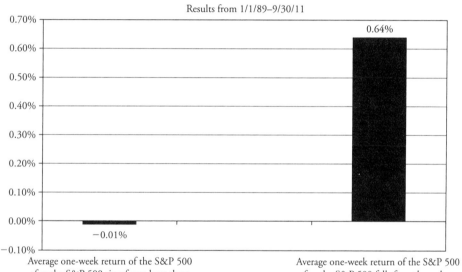

Results from 1/1/89–9/30/11

0.64%

−0.01%

Average one-week return of the S&P 500 after the S&P 500 rises for at least three days in a row

Average one-week return of the S&P 500 after the S&P 500 falls for at least three days in a row

FIGURE 4.4 Nasdaq 100: An Up Day in the Nasdaq Has Slightly Outperformed a Down Day in the Nasdaq after One Week

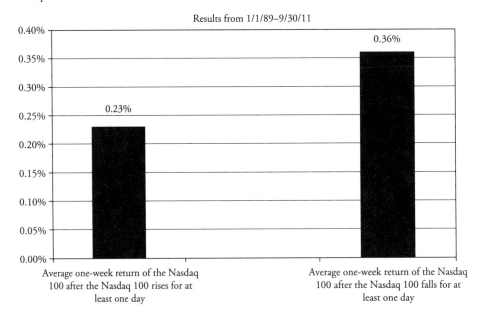

Results from 1/1/89–9/30/11

FIGURE 4.5 Nasdaq 100: Two Down Days in a Row in the Nasdaq Outperformed Two Up Days in a Row after One Week

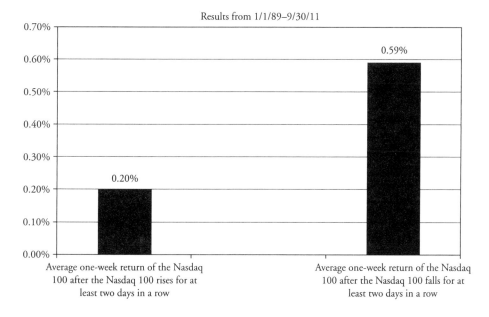

Results from 1/1/89–9/30/11

FIGURE 4.6 Nasdaq 100: Three Down Days in a Row Have Outperformed Three Up Days in a Row in the Nasdaq by an Almost 4-1 Margin after One Week

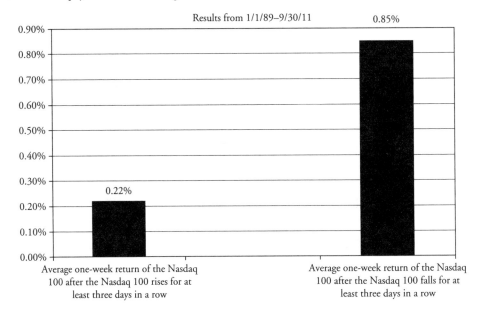

FIGURE 4.7 Time Graph Performance Comparison: S&P 500 Index Buying after Prices Rise for One Day versus Falling for One Day

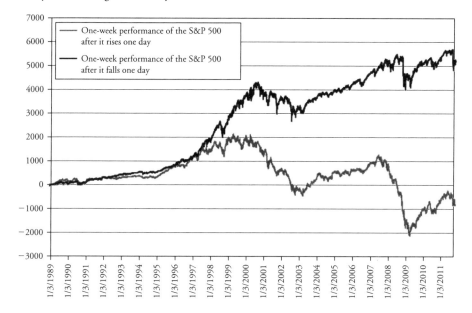

FIGURE 4.8 Time Graph Performance Comparison: S&P 500 Index Buying after Prices Rise for Two Days in a Row versus Falling for Two Days in a Row

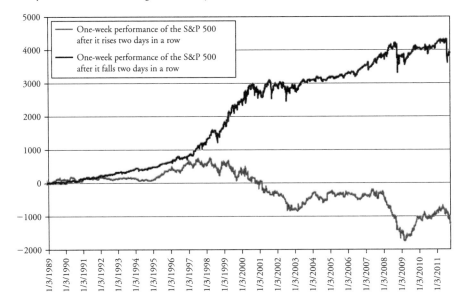

FIGURE 4.9 Time Graph Performance Comparison: S&P 500 Index Buying after Prices Rise for Three Days in a Row versus Falling for Three Days in a Row

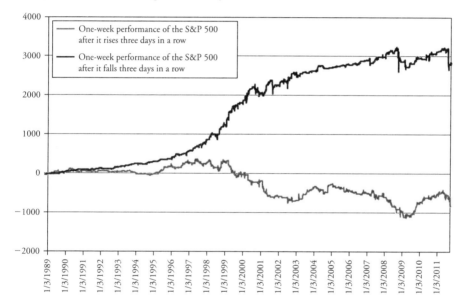

FIGURE 4.10 Time Graph Performance Comparison: Nasdaq 100 Index Buying after Prices Rise for One Day versus Falling for One Day

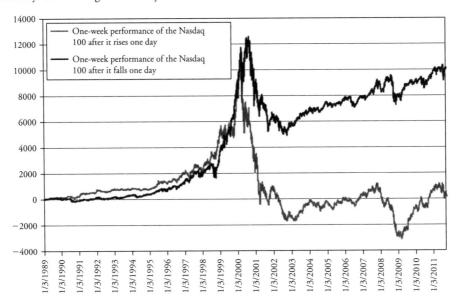

FIGURE 4.11 Time Graph Performance Comparison: Nasdaq 100 Index Buying after Prices Rise for Two Days in a Row versus Falling for Two Days in a Row

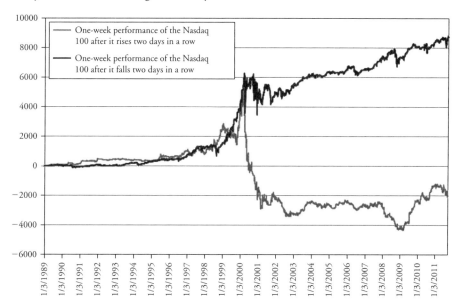

FIGURE 4.12 Time Graph Performance Comparison: Nasdaq 100 Index Buying after Prices Rise for Three Days in a Row versus Falling for Three Days in a Row

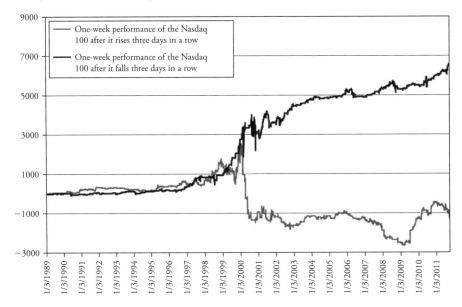

TABLE 4.1 SPX Up Days in a Row versus Down Days in a Row (1/1/1989 to 9/30/2011)

Index	Rule 1	Rule 2	Time Period	Gain/Loss	# Winners	# Days	% Profitable	Benchmark Average	% Profitable Benchmark
SP500	After 1 up day		1 day	0.01	1603	3064	52.32	0.03	53.43
SP500	After 1 up day		2 days	0.02	1648	3063	53.8	0.06	53.92
SP500	After 1 up day		1 week	0.06	1710	3061	55.86	0.15	56.19
SP500	After 2 up days		1 day	0	821	1603	51.22	0.03	53.43
SP500	After 2 up days		2 days	0	858	1603	53.52	0.06	53.92
SP500	After 2 up days		1 week	0.01	896	1601	55.97	0.15	56.19
SP500	After 3 up days		1 day	−0.02	397	821	48.36	0.03	53.43
SP500	After 3 up days		2 days	−0.05	420	821	51.16	0.06	53.92
SP500	After 3 up days		1 week	−0.01	474	820	57.8	0.15	56.19
SP500	After 1 down day		1 day	0.06	1460	2667	54.74	0.03	53.43
SP500	After 1 down day		2 days	0.11	1442	2667	54.07	0.06	53.92
SP500	After 1 down day		1 week	0.27	1508	2666	56.56	0.15	56.19
SP500	After 2 down days		1 day	0.09	675	1206	55.97	0.03	53.43
SP500	After 2 down days		2 days	0.21	680	1206	56.38	0.06	53.92
SP500	After 2 down days		1 week	0.41	698	1206	57.88	0.15	56.19
SP500	After 3 down days		1 day	0.21	326	529	61.63	0.03	53.43
SP500	After 3 down days		2 days	0.37	322	529	60.87	0.06	53.92
SP500	After 3 down days		1 week	0.64	328	529	62	0.15	56.19
SP500	After 1 up day	Above 200-day MA	1 day	0.04	1223	2292	53.36	0.04	54.12
SP500	After 1 up day	Above 200-day MA	2 days	0.08	1272	2292	55.5	0.08	55.29
SP500	After 1 up day	Above 200-day MA	1 week	0.15	1314	2292	57.33	0.19	57.22

(continued)

57

TABLE 4.1 (*Continued*)

Index	Rule 1	Rule 2	Time Period	Gain/Loss	# Winners	# Days	% Profitable	Benchmark Average	% Profitable Benchmark
SP500	After 2 up days	Above 200-day MA	1 day	0.04	655	1258	52.07	0.04	54.12
SP500	After 2 up days	Above 200-day MA	2 days	0.08	695	1258	55.25	0.08	55.29
SP500	After 2 up days	Above 200-day MA	1 week	0.11	723	1258	57.47	0.19	57.22
SP500	After 3 up days	Above 200-day MA	1 day	0.02	332	672	49.4	0.04	54.12
SP500	After 3 up days	Above 200-day MA	2 days	0.05	358	672	53.27	0.08	55.29
SP500	After 3 up days	Above 200-day MA	1 week	0.1	395	672	58.78	0.19	57.22
SP500	After 1 down day	Above 200-day MA	1 day	0.03	990	1797	55.09	0.04	54.12
SP500	After 1 down day	Above 200-day MA	2 days	0.08	989	1797	55.04	0.08	55.29
SP500	After 1 down day	Above 200-day MA	1 week	0.25	1025	1797	57.04	0.19	57.22
SP500	After 2 down days	Above 200-day MA	1 day	0.03	430	768	55.99	0.04	54.12
SP500	After 2 down days	Above 200-day MA	2 days	0.15	442	768	57.55	0.08	55.29
SP500	After 2 down days	Above 200-day MA	1 week	0.36	447	768	58.2	0.19	57.22
SP500	After 3 down days	Above 200-day MA	1 day	0.17	201	317	63.41	0.04	54.12
SP500	After 3 down days	Above 200-day MA	2 days	0.37	198	317	62.46	0.08	55.29
SP500	After 3 down days	Above 200-day MA	1 week	0.66	205	317	64.67	0.19	57.22
SP500	After 1 up day	Below 200-day MA	1 day	-0.09	380	772	49.22	0.01	51.7
SP500	After 1 up day	Below 200-day MA	2 days	-0.16	376	771	48.77	0.02	50.52
SP500	After 1 up day	Below 200-day MA	1 week	-0.21	396	769	51.5	0.06	53.6
SP500	After 2 up days	Below 200-day MA	1 day	-0.14	166	345	48.12	0.01	51.7
SP500	After 2 up days	Below 200-day MA	2 days	-0.26	163	345	47.25	0.02	50.52
SP500	After 2 up days	Below 200-day MA	1 week	-0.35	173	343	50.44	0.06	53.6

SP500	After 3 up days	Below 200-day MA	1 day	−0.24	65	149	43.62	0.01	51.7
SP500	After 3 up days	Below 200-day MA	2 days	−0.52	62	149	41.61	0.02	50.52
SP500	After 3 up days	Below 200-day MA	1 week	−0.49	79	148	53.38	0.06	53.6
SP500	After 1 down day	Below 200-day MA	1 day	0.11	470	870	54.02	0.01	51.7
SP500	After 1 down day	Below 200-day MA	2 days	0.18	453	870	52.07	0.02	50.52
SP500	After 1 down day	Below 200-day MA	1 week	0.3	483	869	55.58	0.06	53.6
SP500	After 2 down days	Below 200-day MA	1 day	0.2	245	438	55.94	0.01	51.7
SP500	After 2 down days	Below 200-day MA	2 days	0.3	238	438	54.34	0.02	50.52
SP500	After 2 down days	Below 200-day MA	1 week	0.5	251	438	57.31	0.06	53.6
SP500	After 3 down days	Below 200-day MA	1 day	0.27	125	212	58.96	0.01	51.7
SP500	After 3 down days	Below 200-day MA	2 days	0.36	124	212	58.49	0.02	50.52
SP500	After 3 down days	Below 200-day MA	1 week	0.62	123	212	58.02	0.06	53.6

TABLE 4.2 NDX Up Days in a Row versus Down Days in a Row (1/1/1989 to 9/30/2011)

Index	Rule 1	Rule 2	Time Period	Gain/Loss	# Winners	# Days	% Profitable	Benchmark Average	% Profitable Benchmark
NDX100	After 1 up day		1 day	0.08	1720	3112	55.27	0.06	54.26
NDX100	After 1 up day		2 days	0.08	1691	3112	54.34	0.12	53.54
NDX100	After 1 up day		1 week	0.23	1746	3110	56.14	0.29	56.17
NDX100	After 2 up days		1 day	0.05	945	1720	54.94	0.06	54.26
NDX100	After 2 up days		2 days	0.08	940	1720	54.65	0.12	53.54
NDX100	After 2 up days		1 week	0.2	965	1718	56.17	0.29	56.17
NDX100	After 3 up days		1 day	0.06	523	945	55.34	0.06	54.26
NDX100	After 3 up days		2 days	0.06	512	945	54.18	0.12	53.54
NDX100	After 3 up days		1 week	0.22	533	944	56.46	0.29	56.17
NDX100	After 1 down day		1 day	0.04	1388	2615	53.08	0.06	54.26
NDX100	After 1 down day		2 days	0.16	1375	2614	52.6	0.12	53.54
NDX100	After 1 down day		1 week	0.36	1467	2613	56.14	0.29	56.17
NDX100	After 2 down days		1 day	0.15	664	1224	54.25	0.06	54.26
NDX100	After 2 down days		2 days	0.34	667	1223	54.54	0.12	53.54
NDX100	After 2 down days		1 week	0.59	702	1223	57.4	0.29	56.17
NDX100	After 3 down days		1 day	0.34	320	558	57.35	0.06	54.26
NDX100	After 3 down days		2 days	0.51	324	558	58.06	0.12	53.54
NDX100	After 3 down days		1 week	0.85	337	558	60.39	0.29	56.17
NDX100	After 1 up day	Above 200-day MA	1 day	0.1	1309	2335	56.06	0.07	54.97
NDX100	After 1 up day	Above 200-day MA	2 days	0.15	1300	2335	55.67	0.14	54.62
NDX100	After 1 up day	Above 200-day MA	1 week	0.35	1348	2335	57.73	0.36	57.34

60

NDX100	After 2 up days	Above 200-day MA	1 day	0.06	751	1349	55.67	0.07	54.97
NDX100	After 2 up days	Above 200-day MA	2 days	0.13	750	1349	55.6	0.14	54.62
NDX100	After 2 up days	Above 200-day MA	1 week	0.31	778	1349	57.67	0.36	57.34
NDX100	After 3 up days	Above 200-day MA	1 day	0.08	433	768	56.38	0.07	54.97
NDX100	After 3 up days	Above 200-day MA	2 days	0.13	421	768	54.82	0.14	54.62
NDX100	After 3 up days	Above 200-day MA	1 week	0.32	449	768	58.46	0.36	57.34
NDX100	After 1 down day	Above 200-day MA	1 day	0.03	934	1747	53.46	0.07	54.97
NDX100	After 1 down day	Above 200-day MA	2 days	0.13	929	1747	53.18	0.14	54.62
NDX100	After 1 down day	Above 200-day MA	1 week	0.36	991	1747	56.73	0.36	57.34
NDX100	After 2 down days	Above 200-day MA	1 day	0.05	411	766	53.66	0.07	54.97
NDX100	After 2 down days	Above 200-day MA	2 days	0.26	415	766	54.18	0.14	54.62
NDX100	After 2 down days	Above 200-day MA	1 week	0.45	438	766	57.18	0.36	57.34
NDX100	After 3 down days	Above 200-day MA	1 day	0.23	190	330	57.58	0.07	54.97
NDX100	After 3 down days	Above 200-day MA	2 days	0.51	194	330	58.79	0.14	54.62
NDX100	After 3 down days	Above 200-day MA	1 week	0.62	198	330	60	0.36	57.34
NDX100	After 1 up day	Below 200-day MA	1 day	0.02	411	777	52.9	0.04	52.52
NDX100	After 1 up day	Below 200-day MA	2 days	−0.11	391	777	50.32	0.06	50.85
NDX100	After 1 up day	Below 200-day MA	1 week	−0.12	398	775	51.35	0.14	53.26
NDX100	After 2 up days	Below 200-day MA	1 day	0.03	194	371	52.29	0.04	52.52
NDX100	After 2 up days	Below 200-day MA	2 days	−0.12	190	371	51.21	0.06	50.85
NDX100	After 2 up days	Below 200-day MA	1 week	−0.17	187	369	50.68	0.14	53.26
NDX100	After 3 up days	Below 200-day MA	1 day	−0.03	90	177	50.85	0.04	52.52
NDX100	After 3 up days	Below 200-day MA	2 days	−0.23	91	177	51.41	0.06	50.85
NDX100	After 3 up days	Below 200-day MA	1 week	−0.24	84	176	47.73	0.14	53.26

(continued)

TABLE 4.2 (*Continued*)

Index	Rule 1	Rule 2	Time Period	Gain/Loss	# Winners	# Days	% Profitable	Benchmark Average	% Profitable Benchmark
NDX100	After 1 down day	Below 200-day MA	1 day	0.06	454	868	52.3	0.04	52.52
NDX100	After 1 down day	Below 200-day MA	2 days	0.23	446	867	51.44	0.06	50.85
NDX100	After 1 down day	Below 200-day MA	1 week	0.37	476	866	54.97	0.14	53.26
NDX100	After 2 down days	Below 200-day MA	1 day	0.31	253	458	55.24	0.04	52.52
NDX100	After 2 down days	Below 200-day MA	2 days	0.48	252	457	55.14	0.06	50.85
NDX100	After 2 down days	Below 200-day MA	1 week	0.81	264	457	57.77	0.14	53.26
NDX100	After 3 down days	Below 200-day MA	1 day	0.5	130	228	57.02	0.04	52.52
NDX100	After 3 down days	Below 200-day MA	2 days	0.52	130	228	57.02	0.06	50.85
NDX100	After 3 down days	Below 200-day MA	1 week	1.19	139	228	60.96	0.14	53.26

Summary and Conclusion

The notion that short-term market strength follows through with more strength again appears to be wrong. In fact, the results show fairly conclusively that short-term weakness is followed by short-term strength, and short-term strength is followed by short-term underperformance. This again leads to the conclusion that, should these results continue to hold true in the future, *waiting for a market to decline multiple days in a row is better than buying into strength.*

Let's now look at how the market has performed during extreme levels of daily advancing and declining issues.

CHAPTER 5

Market Breadth

Nearly every night of the business week, the financial press reports the number of stocks that have advanced versus the number of stocks that have declined for the day. "Advancing issues led declining issues by a 2-1 margin." "Declining issues outnumbered advancing issues 2076 to 1103." And usually the bigger the difference in the two numbers, the more likely you will hear adjectives used such as "healthy" to describe the good days and "poor" to describe the days that declining issues far outnumber the advancing issues. On the days that the numbers are truly far apart, you'll undoubtedly hear analysts telling you just how good things are because so many more stocks rose for the day, and they'll tell you just how weak things look when so many more stocks declined for the day.

This type of analysis seems logical, doesn't it? More stocks rising supposedly means strong market breadth and a broad-based rally. And more stocks declining in price for the day means weakness. And supposedly this weakness is a bad sign. This attitude and interpretation of daily price movement is among the most prevalent thought processes found on Wall Street.

We looked at a 15+-year period from 8/1/1996 to 9/30/2011. The market over that time rose strongly through 1999, then declined sharply through 2002, then recovered in 2003 and rallied through 2007, then had a steep decline in 2008, and then rallied again into 2011. It saw both bull moves and bear moves.

We looked at market breadth in two distinct ways. First, we looked at advancing issues being greater than declining issues for multiple days in a row. Conventional wisdom is that the more days advancing issues exceed declining issues, the stronger the market internals are. The opposite is supposedly true for when declining issues exceed advancing issues for a number of days. When this occurs, the market is showing weakness, and this weakness is interpreted as negative for the near future.

Our second test looked at the days when advancing issues outnumbered declining issues by a 2-1 margin and a 3-1 margin. When this happens, it means the rally is broad-based, and analysts usually tell you it's a very healthy sign. The opposite occurs when declining issues outnumber advancing issues by a 2-1 and 3-1 margin. Reportedly, things are bleak, and it's interpreted as a bad sign.

Let's now look at the results. As you will see, the results are clear-cut.

Consecutive Days of Declining Issues Greater than Advancing Issues on the NYSE Has Led to Higher Prices Short-Term

1. The first thing that is apparent is that multiple days of declining issues greater than advancing issues for both the S&P 500 index (SPX) and the Nasdaq 100 index (NDX) not only outperformed the benchmark over the next week, but they also outperformed the times when there were multiple days of advancing issues greater than declining issues. For example, look at the NDX when declining issues outnumbered advancing issues two days in a row. Over the next week, the average gain was 0.51 percent. When advancing issues were greater than declining issues two days in a row in the NDX, the market gained only 0.03 percent over the next week. We see the same type of results for three days, and we see the same type of results in the SPX. There is a consistent theme here . . . multiple days of declining issues being greater than advancing issues is not a sign of future weakness. It's a sign that a rally is likely near, and at least over the 15+ years tested, this rally has been stronger than average.

Significant Underperformance Occurs When Advancing Issues Outnumber Declining Issues and the Market Is Trading under Its 200-Day Moving Average

2. When you look at advancing issues greater than declining issues when the market is under its 200-day moving average, the results become even more obvious. Some of the losses during this time are significant and underperform the average one-week hold even further.

Poor Breadth Days Outperformed Strong Breadth Days

3. We then looked at the times when advancing issues outnumbered declining issues by a 2-1 margin and a 3-1 margin. These are the times when the market is supposedly strong and healthy. Again, the results show this not to be true. When advancing issues outnumber declining issues by a 2-1 margin, the market lost money over the next week for the SPX. When declining issues outnumbered advancing issues by a 2-1 and 3-1 margin, the following week has seen gains as the market, on average, rose. And, when you match things up, it's obvious that at least from August 1996 to September 2011, you would have been better off being a buyer after these supposedly bad days versus being a buyer when breadth was strong.

See *Table Explanation* at the beginning of this book for column descriptions.

FIGURE 5.1 S&P 500: Days with 2:1 Decliners Outperformed Days with 2:1 Advancers

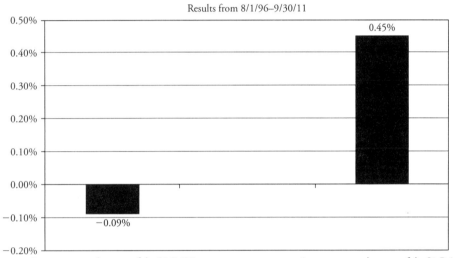

Results from 8/1/96–9/30/11

Average one-week return of the S&P 500 when NYSE Advancers are at least two times NYSE Decliners today

Average one-week return of the S&P 500 when NYSE Decliners are at least two times NYSE Advancers today

FIGURE 5.2   S&P 500: The Market (on Average) Has Lost Money within a Week Following Days When Advancing Issues Outnumbered Declining Issues by at Least 3:1

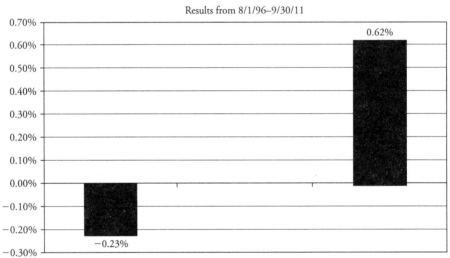

Results from 8/1/96–9/30/11

FIGURE 5.3 S&P 500: Two Consecutive Days of Declining Issues Outnumbering Advancing Issues Has Outperformed Two Consecutive Days of Advancing Issues Outnumbering Declining Issues

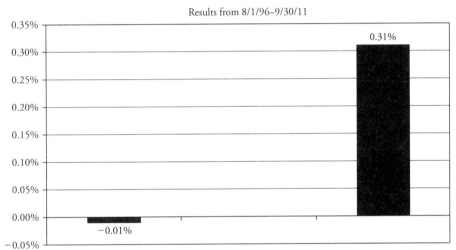

Results from 8/1/96–9/30/11

FIGURE 5.4   S&P 500: Three Consecutive Days of Declining Issues Greater than Advancing Issues Have Strongly Outperformed Three Consecutive Days of Advancing Issues Greater than Declining

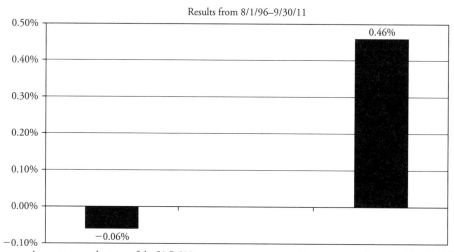

Results from 8/1/96–9/30/11

Average one-week return of the S&P 500 when NYSE Advancers are greater than NYSE Decliners for at least three days in a row

Average one-week return of the S&P 500 when NYSE Advancers are less than NYSE Decliners for at least three days in a row

FIGURE 5.5 Time Graph Performance Comparison: S&P 500 Index Advancers Are Greater than Two Times Decliners versus Decliners Greater than Two Times Advancers

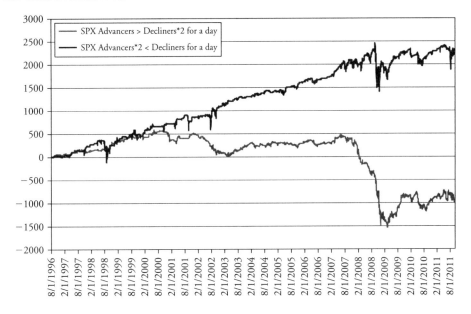

FIGURE 5.6 Time Graph Performance Comparison: S&P 500 Index Advancers Are Greater than Three Times Decliners versus Decliners Greater than Three Times Advancers

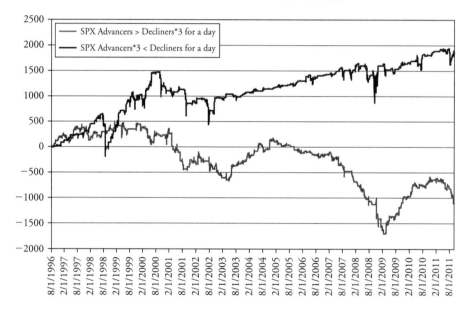

FIGURE 5.7 Time Graph Performance Comparison: Nasdaq 100 Index Advancers Are Greater than Two Times Decliners versus Decliners Greater than Two Times Advancers

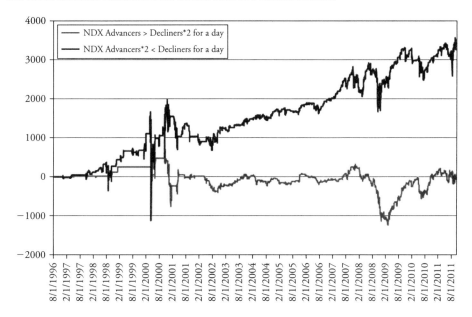

FIGURE 5.8 Time Graph Performance Comparison: Nasdaq 100 Index Advancers Are Greater than Three Times Decliners versus Decliners Greater than Three Times Advancers

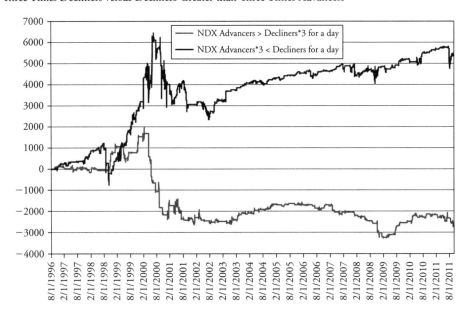

TABLE 5.1 SPX Market Breadth (8/1/1996 to 9/30/2011)

Index	Rule 1	Rule 2	Time Period	Gain/Loss	# Winners	# Days	% Profitable	Benchmark Average	% Profitable Benchmark
SP500	Adv > 2*Dec for one day		1 day	−0.03	346	655	52.82	0.02	53.06
SP500	Adv > 2*Dec for one day		2 days	−0.11	342	654	52.29	0.05	53.55
SP500	Adv > 2*Dec for one day		1 week	−0.09	358	652	54.91	0.11	54.82
SP500	Adv > 3*Dec for one day		1 day	−0.16	115	240	47.92	0.02	53.06
SP500	Adv > 3*Dec for one day		2 days	−0.27	125	240	52.08	0.05	53.55
SP500	Adv > 3*Dec for one day		1 week	−0.23	133	239	55.65	0.11	54.82
SP500	Adv*2 < Dec for one day		1 day	0.15	312	550	56.73	0.02	53.06
SP500	Adv*2 < Dec for one day		2 days	0.27	295	550	53.64	0.05	53.55
SP500	Adv*2 < Dec for one day		1 week	0.45	315	549	57.38	0.11	54.82
SP500	Adv*3 < Dec for one day		1 day	0.23	148	248	59.68	0.02	53.06
SP500	Adv*3 < Dec for one day		2 days	0.34	133	248	53.63	0.05	53.55
SP500	Adv*3 < Dec for one day		1 week	0.62	141	247	57.09	0.11	54.82
SP500	Adv > Dec for 1 day		1 day	0.02	1106	2092	52.87	0.02	53.06
SP500	Adv > Dec for 1 day		2 days	0.01	1134	2091	54.23	0.05	53.55
SP500	Adv > Dec for 1 day		1 week	0.04	1145	2089	54.81	0.11	54.82
SP500	Adv > Dec for 2 days		1 day	0	654	1240	52.74	0.02	53.06
SP500	Adv > Dec for 2 days		2 days	0.02	688	1240	55.48	0.05	53.55
SP500	Adv > Dec for 2 days		1 week	−0.01	662	1238	53.47	0.11	54.82
SP500	Adv > Dec for 3 days		1 day	0.02	391	742	52.7	0.02	53.06
SP500	Adv > Dec for 3 days		2 days	0.02	413	742	55.66	0.05	53.55
SP500	Adv > Dec for 3 days		1 week	−0.06	395	741	53.31	0.11	54.82

(continued)

75

TABLE 5.1 (*Continued*)

Index	Rule 1	Rule 2	Time Period	Gain/Loss	# Winners	# Days	% Profitable	Benchmark Average	% Profitable Benchmark
SP500	Adv < Dec for 1 day		1 day	0.02	919	1724	53.31	0.02	53.06
SP500	Adv < Dec for 1 day		2 days	0.09	910	1724	52.78	0.05	53.55
SP500	Adv < Dec for 1 day		1 week	0.19	946	1723	54.9	0.11	54.82
SP500	Adv < Dec for 2 days		1 day	0.07	473	872	54.24	0.02	53.06
SP500	Adv < Dec for 2 days		2 days	0.19	482	872	55.28	0.05	53.55
SP500	Adv < Dec for 2 days		1 week	0.31	482	872	55.28	0.11	54.82
SP500	Adv < Dec for 3 days		1 day	0.19	264	453	58.28	0.02	53.06
SP500	Adv < Dec for 3 days		2 days	0.26	258	453	56.95	0.05	53.55
SP500	Adv < Dec for 3 days		1 week	0.46	255	453	56.29	0.11	54.82
SP500	Adv > Dec for 1 day	Above 200-day MA	1 day	0.07	788	1442	54.65	0.03	54.2
SP500	Adv > Dec for 1 day	Above 200-day MA	2 days	0.11	828	1442	57.42	0.07	55.56
SP500	Adv > Dec for 1 day	Above 200-day MA	1 week	0.2	829	1442	57.49	0.18	56.44
SP500	Adv > Dec for 2 days	Above 200-day MA	1 day	0.06	487	894	54.47	0.03	54.2
SP500	Adv > Dec for 2 days	Above 200-day MA	2 days	0.11	527	894	58.95	0.07	55.56
SP500	Adv > Dec for 2 days	Above 200-day MA	1 week	0.17	506	894	56.6	0.18	56.44
SP500	Adv > Dec for 3 days	Above 200-day MA	1 day	0.06	295	556	53.06	0.03	54.2
SP500	Adv > Dec for 3 days	Above 200-day MA	2 days	0.13	331	556	59.53	0.07	55.56
SP500	Adv > Dec for 3 days	Above 200-day MA	1 week	0.16	310	556	55.76	0.18	56.44
SP500	Adv < Dec for 1 day	Above 200-day MA	1 day	−0.01	571	1065	53.62	0.03	54.2
SP500	Adv < Dec for 1 day	Above 200-day MA	2 days	0.04	566	1065	53.15	0.07	55.56
SP500	Adv < Dec for 1 day	Above 200-day MA	1 week	0.15	587	1065	55.12	0.18	56.44
SP500	Adv < Dec for 2 days	Above 200-day MA	1 day	0.02	282	518	54.44	0.03	54.2

SP500	Adv < Dec for 2 days	Above 200-day MA	2 days	0.1	291	518	56.18	0.07	55.56
SP500	Adv < Dec for 2 days	Above 200-day MA	1 week	0.2	291	518	56.18	0.18	56.44
SP500	Adv < Dec for 3 days	Above 200-day MA	1 day	0.14	152	255	59.61	0.03	54.2
SP500	Adv < Dec for 3 days	Above 200-day MA	2 days	0.23	150	255	58.82	0.07	55.56
SP500	Adv < Dec for 3 days	Above 200-day MA	1 week	0.3	147	255	57.65	0.18	56.44
SP500	Adv > Dec for 1 day	Below 200-day MA	1 day	−0.07	318	650	48.92	0	50.88
SP500	Adv > Dec for 1 day	Below 200-day MA	2 days	−0.19	306	649	47.15	−0.01	49.69
SP500	Adv > Dec for 1 day	Below 200-day MA	1 week	−0.31	316	647	48.84	−0.02	51.72
SP500	Adv > Dec for 2 days	Below 200-day MA	1 day	−0.15	167	346	48.27	0	50.88
SP500	Adv > Dec for 2 days	Below 200-day MA	2 days	−0.22	161	346	46.53	−0.01	49.69
SP500	Adv > Dec for 2 days	Below 200-day MA	1 week	−0.51	156	344	45.35	−0.02	51.72
SP500	Adv > Dec for 3 days	Below 200-day MA	1 day	−0.07	96	186	51.61	0	50.88
SP500	Adv > Dec for 3 days	Below 200-day MA	2 days	−0.32	82	186	44.09	−0.01	49.69
SP500	Adv > Dec for 3 days	Below 200-day MA	1 week	−0.72	85	185	45.95	−0.02	51.72
SP500	Adv < Dec for 1 day	Below 200-day MA	1 day	0.07	348	659	52.81	0	50.88
SP500	Adv < Dec for 1 day	Below 200-day MA	2 days	0.17	344	659	52.2	−0.01	49.69
SP500	Adv < Dec for 1 day	Below 200-day MA	1 week	0.27	359	658	54.56	−0.02	51.72
SP500	Adv < Dec for 2 days	Below 200-day MA	1 day	0.15	191	354	53.95	0	50.88
SP500	Adv < Dec for 2 days	Below 200-day MA	2 days	0.33	191	354	53.95	−0.01	49.69
SP500	Adv < Dec for 2 days	Below 200-day MA	1 week	0.46	191	354	53.95	−0.02	51.72
SP500	Adv < Dec for 3 days	Below 200-day MA	1 day	0.25	112	198	56.57	0	50.88
SP500	Adv < Dec for 3 days	Below 200-day MA	2 days	0.31	108	198	54.55	−0.01	49.69
SP500	Adv < Dec for 3 days	Below 200-day MA	1 week	0.66	108	198	54.55	−0.02	51.72

TABLE 5.2 NDX Market Breadth (8/1/1996 to 9/30/2011)

Index	Rule 1	Rule 2	Time Period	Gain/Loss	# Winners	# Days	% Profitable	Benchmark Average	% Profitable Benchmark
NDX100	Adv > 2*Dec for one day		1 day	−0.08	194	372	52.15	0.05	54.09
NDX100	Adv > 2*Dec for one day		2 days	−0.09	202	372	54.3	0.1	53.08
NDX100	Adv > 2*Dec for one day		1 week	0.05	212	371	57.14	0.25	55.32
NDX100	Adv > 3*Dec for one day		1 day	−0.29	47	98	47.96	0.05	54.09
NDX100	Adv > 3*Dec for one day		2 days	−0.45	47	98	47.96	0.1	53.08
NDX100	Adv > 3*Dec for one day		1 week	0.15	55	98	56.12	0.25	55.32
NDX100	Adv*2 < Dec for one day		1 day	0.22	309	556	55.58	0.05	54.09
NDX100	Adv*2 < Dec for one day		2 days	0.27	294	556	52.88	0.1	53.08
NDX100	Adv*2 < Dec for one day		1 week	0.49	307	555	55.32	0.25	55.32
NDX100	Adv*3 < Dec for one day		1 day	0.43	115	204	56.37	0.05	54.09
NDX100	Adv*3 < Dec for one day		2 days	0.54	111	204	54.41	0.1	53.08
NDX100	Adv*3 < Dec for one day		1 week	0.79	114	203	56.16	0.25	55.32
NDX100	Adv > Dec for 1 day		1 day	0.01	1003	1851	54.19	0.05	54.09
NDX100	Adv > Dec for 1 day		2 days	0	987	1850	53.35	0.1	53.08
NDX100	Adv > Dec for 1 day		1 week	0.11	1025	1848	55.47	0.25	55.32
NDX100	Adv > Dec for 2 days		1 day	−0.03	506	962	52.6	0.05	54.09
NDX100	Adv > Dec for 2 days		2 days	0	518	962	53.85	0.1	53.08
NDX100	Adv > Dec for 2 days		1 week	0.03	525	960	54.69	0.25	55.32
NDX100	Adv > Dec for 3 days		1 day	0.01	270	495	54.55	0.05	54.09
NDX100	Adv > Dec for 3 days		2 days	0.05	284	495	57.37	0.1	53.08
NDX100	Adv > Dec for 3 days		1 week	−0.02	270	494	54.66	0.25	55.32
NDX100	Adv < Dec for 1 day		1 day	0.1	1059	1962	53.98	0.05	54.09

NDX100	Adv < Dec for 1 day		2 days	0.2	1038	1962	52.91	0.1	53.08
NDX100	Adv < Dec for 1 day		1 week	0.38	1082	1961	55.18	0.25	55.32
NDX100	Adv < Dec for 2 days		1 day	0.15	590	1074	54.93	0.05	54.09
NDX100	Adv < Dec for 2 days		2 days	0.24	561	1074	52.23	0.1	53.08
NDX100	Adv < Dec for 2 days		1 week	0.51	594	1074	55.31	0.25	55.32
NDX100	Adv < Dec for 3 days		1 day	0.25	344	604	56.95	0.05	54.09
NDX100	Adv < Dec for 3 days		2 days	0.34	320	604	52.98	0.1	53.08
NDX100	Adv < Dec for 3 days		1 week	0.68	338	604	55.96	0.25	55.32
NDX100	Adv > Dec for 1 day	Above 200-day MA	1 day	0.07	745	1332	55.93	0.07	55.43
NDX100	Adv > Dec for 1 day	Above 200-day MA	2 days	0.12	736	1332	55.26	0.15	54.66
NDX100	Adv > Dec for 1 day	Above 200-day MA	1 week	0.33	775	1332	58.18	0.37	57.25
NDX100	Adv > Dec for 2 days	Above 200-day MA	1 day	0.02	390	726	53.72	0.07	55.43
NDX100	Adv > Dec for 2 days	Above 200-day MA	2 days	0.1	404	726	55.65	0.15	54.66
NDX100	Adv > Dec for 2 days	Above 200-day MA	1 week	0.19	419	726	57.71	0.37	57.25
NDX100	Adv > Dec for 3 days	Above 200-day MA	1 day	0.07	221	390	56.67	0.07	55.43
NDX100	Adv > Dec for 3 days	Above 200-day MA	2 days	0.16	234	390	60	0.15	54.66
NDX100	Adv > Dec for 3 days	Above 200-day MA	1 week	0.15	224	390	57.44	0.37	57.25
NDX100	Adv < Dec for 1 day	Above 200-day MA	1 day	0.07	687	1252	54.87	0.07	55.43
NDX100	Adv < Dec for 1 day	Above 200-day MA	2 days	0.19	677	1252	54.07	0.15	54.66
NDX100	Adv < Dec for 1 day	Above 200-day MA	1 week	0.42	705	1252	56.31	0.37	57.25
NDX100	Adv < Dec for 2 days	Above 200-day MA	1 day	0.07	356	643	55.37	0.07	55.43
NDX100	Adv < Dec for 2 days	Above 200-day MA	2 days	0.17	334	643	51.94	0.15	54.66
NDX100	Adv < Dec for 2 days	Above 200-day MA	1 week	0.39	360	643	55.99	0.37	57.25
NDX100	Adv < Dec for 3 days	Above 200-day MA	1 day	0.08	186	332	56.02	0.07	55.43

(continued)

TABLE 5.2 *(Continued)*

Index	Rule 1	Rule 2	Time Period	Gain/Loss	# Winners	# Days	% Profitable	Benchmark Average	% Profitable Benchmark
NDX100	Adv < Dec for 3 days	Above 200-day MA	2 days	0.22	174	332	52.41	0.15	54.66
NDX100	Adv < Dec for 3 days	Above 200-day MA	1 week	0.4	188	332	56.63	0.37	57.25
NDX100	Adv > Dec for 1 day	Below 200-day MA	1 day	−0.14	258	519	49.71	0.02	51.26
NDX100	Adv > Dec for 1 day	Below 200-day MA	2 days	−0.29	251	518	48.46	0	49.76
NDX100	Adv > Dec for 1 day	Below 200-day MA	1 week	−0.46	250	516	48.45	−0.02	51.26
NDX100	Adv > Dec for 2 days	Below 200-day MA	1 day	−0.19	116	236	49.15	0.02	51.26
NDX100	Adv > Dec for 2 days	Below 200-day MA	2 days	−0.29	114	236	48.31	0	49.76
NDX100	Adv > Dec for 2 days	Below 200-day MA	1 week	−0.46	106	234	45.3	−0.02	51.26
NDX100	Adv > Dec for 3 days	Below 200-day MA	1 day	−0.25	49	105	46.67	0.02	51.26
NDX100	Adv > Dec for 3 days	Below 200-day MA	2 days	−0.33	50	105	47.62	0	49.76
NDX100	Adv > Dec for 3 days	Below 200-day MA	1 week	−0.66	46	104	44.23	−0.02	51.26
NDX100	Adv < Dec for 1 day	Below 200-day MA	1 day	0.14	372	710	52.39	0.02	51.26
NDX100	Adv < Dec for 1 day	Below 200-day MA	2 days	0.22	361	710	50.85	0	49.76
NDX100	Adv < Dec for 1 day	Below 200-day MA	1 week	0.3	377	709	53.17	−0.02	51.26
NDX100	Adv < Dec for 2 days	Below 200-day MA	1 day	0.27	234	431	54.29	0.02	51.26
NDX100	Adv < Dec for 2 days	Below 200-day MA	2 days	0.35	227	431	52.67	0	49.76
NDX100	Adv < Dec for 2 days	Below 200-day MA	1 week	0.7	234	431	54.29	−0.02	51.26
NDX100	Adv < Dec for 3 days	Below 200-day MA	1 day	0.46	158	272	58.09	0.02	51.26
NDX100	Adv < Dec for 3 days	Below 200-day MA	2 days	0.49	146	272	53.68	0	49.76
NDX100	Adv < Dec for 3 days	Below 200-day MA	1 week	1.02	150	272	55.15	−0.02	51.26

Summary and Conclusion

These results are at odds with the way the majority of Wall Street interprets advancing and declining issues, and is at odds with the way the financial markets press reports the news. Whether these findings will hold in the future is hard to say, but they philosophically and statistically fall in line with many of the other tests published here.

In conclusion, these results show that it has been better to be selectively buying the SPX and the NDX when market breadth has been poor versus when market breadth has been strong.

We'll now move to looking at market volume and its relationship to price movement.

CHAPTER 6

Volume

We are aware of many books and articles written on the role that volume plays in predicting short-term movement in stock prices, but we are not aware of many statistical studies to back these claims. This is surprising considering how popular volume is as an indicator and just how much it is relied upon by traders and investors. In this chapter, we look at a combination of volume and price in order to see if there is an edge.

In many sections in this book, we found evidence that the setup or indicator used has led to an edge in the markets over the past one to two decades. Interestingly, in looking at volume, which is an indicator that is most often quoted by the media and many professionals, the results were mixed. We know these findings will be of most interest because many traders use volume to interpret and identify trading situations. Based upon the test data presented next, we were surprised to find these inconsistent results and there was no discernible edge.

A summary of our findings is as follows.

Large Volume Days Alone Are Insignificant

1. If you look at the average daily gain of the S&P 500 (SPX) and the Nasdaq 100 (NDX) on the day that has the highest volume in a week, you'll see insignificant differences. The one-day SPX return was the same as the average daily return but the one-day NDX return was well under the average. The one-week SPX return was near the average return. Both the weekly S&P 500 and NDX returns came in under the overall average. Mixed results here and certainly no clear evidence of any edge looking only at days with big volume.
2. We then looked at the market when it had a large *x*-day volume move and also when the market rose for the day. As you will see, the results were again mixed and led to no obvious conclusions.

3. We looked at the same parameters as #2 except we looked at those days where the market dropped for the day. Again, there was no definitive edge as the returns were inconsistent.

4. In other studies published in this book, when we added a trend component (the 200-day moving average) to the indicator, it often made the results of that indicator better. This was not the case with volume.

See *Table Explanation* at the beginning of this book for column descriptions.

FIGURE 6.1 Time Graph Performance Comparison: S&P 500 Index Has Its Highest Volume Day in a Week and the S&P 500 Rises on that Day versus Falling on that Day

FIGURE 6.2   Time Graph Performance Comparison: Nasdaq 100 Index Has Its Highest Volume Day in a Week and the S&P 500 Rises on that Day versus Falling on that Day

TABLE 6.1 SPX Volume (1/1/1989 to 9/30/2011)

Index	Rule 1	Rule 2	Time Period	Gain/Loss	# Winners	# Days	% Profitable	Benchmark Average	% Profitable Benchmark
SP500	Most volume in 1 week		1 day	0.03	691	1264	54.67	0.03	53.43
SP500	Most volume in 1 week		2 days	0.01	659	1264	52.14	0.06	53.92
SP500	Most volume in 1 week		1 week	0.14	709	1264	56.09	0.15	56.19
SP500	Most volume in 1 month		1 day	0.06	186	348	53.45	0.03	53.43
SP500	Most volume in 1 month		2 days	−0.01	180	348	51.72	0.06	53.92
SP500	Most volume in 1 month		1 week	0.15	184	348	52.87	0.15	56.19
SP500	Most volume in 1 week, market rises today		1 day	0	370	693	53.39	0.03	53.43
SP500	Most volume in 1 week, market rises today		2 days	0.02	364	693	52.53	0.06	53.92
SP500	Most volume in 1 week, market rises today		1 week	0.04	388	693	55.99	0.15	56.19
SP500	Most volume in 1 month, market rises today		1 day	0.07	100	186	53.76	0.03	53.43
SP500	Most volume in 1 month, market rises today		2 days	0.03	99	186	53.23	0.06	53.92
SP500	Most volume in 1 month, market rises today		1 week	0.17	101	186	54.3	0.15	56.19
SP500	Most volume in 1 week, market falls today		1 day	0.06	321	570	56.32	0.03	53.43
SP500	Most volume in 1 week, market falls today		2 days	0.01	295	570	51.75	0.06	53.92
SP500	Most volume in 1 week, market falls today		1 week	0.26	320	570	56.14	0.15	56.19
SP500	Most volume in 1 month, market falls today		1 day	0.06	86	161	53.42	0.03	53.43
SP500	Most volume in 1 month, market falls today		2 days	−0.06	81	161	50.31	0.06	53.92
SP500	Most volume in 1 month, market falls today		1 week	0.13	82	161	50.93	0.15	56.19
SP500	Most volume in 1 week, market rises today	Above 200-day MA	1 day	0.07	294	519	56.65	0.04	54.12
SP500	Most volume in 1 week, market rises today	Above 200-day MA	2 days	0.08	288	519	55.49	0.08	55.29
SP500	Most volume in 1 week, market rises today	Above 200-day MA	1 week	0.15	297	519	57.23	0.19	57.22

(continued)

TABLE 6.1 (Continued)

Index	Rule 1	Rule 2	Time Period	Gain/Loss	# Winners	# Days	% Profitable	Benchmark Average	% Profitable Benchmark
SP500	Most volume in 1 month, market rises today	Above 200-day MA	1 day	0.1	82	148	55.41	0.04	54.12
SP500	Most volume in 1 month, market rises today	Above 200-day MA	2 days	0.09	82	148	55.41	0.08	55.29
SP500	Most volume in 1 month, market rises today	Above 200-day MA	1 week	0.3	84	148	56.76	0.19	57.22
SP500	Most volume in 1 week, market falls today	Above 200-day MA	1 day	−0.02	208	381	54.59	0.04	54.12
SP500	Most volume in 1 week, market falls today	Above 200-day MA	2 days	−0.03	197	381	51.71	0.08	55.29
SP500	Most volume in 1 week, market falls today	Above 200-day MA	1 week	0.3	224	381	58.79	0.19	57.22
SP500	Most volume in 1 month, market falls today	Above 200-day MA	1 day	0.04	50	93	53.76	0.04	54.12
SP500	Most volume in 1 month, market falls today	Above 200-day MA	2 days	0.11	49	93	52.69	0.08	55.29
SP500	Most volume in 1 month, market falls today	Above 200-day MA	1 week	0.42	54	93	58.06	0.19	57.22
SP500	Most volume in 1 week, market rises today	Below 200-day MA	1 day	−0.19	76	174	43.68	0.01	51.7
SP500	Most volume in 1 week, market rises today	Below 200-day MA	2 days	−0.18	76	174	43.68	0.02	50.52
SP500	Most volume in 1 week, market rises today	Below 200-day MA	1 week	−0.3	91	174	52.3	0.06	53.6
SP500	Most volume in 1 month, market rises today	Below 200-day MA	1 day	−0.07	18	38	47.37	0.01	51.7
SP500	Most volume in 1 month, market rises today	Below 200-day MA	2 days	−0.18	17	38	44.74	0.02	50.52
SP500	Most volume in 1 month, market rises today	Below 200-day MA	1 week	−0.33	17	38	44.74	0.06	53.6
SP500	Most volume in 1 week, market falls today	Below 200-day MA	1 day	0.23	113	189	59.79	0.01	51.7
SP500	Most volume in 1 week, market falls today	Below 200-day MA	2 days	0.1	98	189	51.85	0.02	50.52
SP500	Most volume in 1 week, market falls today	Below 200-day MA	1 week	0.17	96	189	50.79	0.06	53.6
SP500	Most volume in 1 month, market falls today	Below 200-day MA	1 day	0.09	36	68	52.94	0.01	51.7
SP500	Most volume in 1 month, market falls today	Below 200-day MA	2 days	−0.29	32	68	47.06	0.02	50.52
SP500	Most volume in 1 month, market falls today	Below 200-day MA	1 week	−0.26	28	68	41.18	0.06	53.6

TABLE 6.2 NDX Volume (9/23/1996 to 9/30/2011)

Index	Rule 1	Rule 2	Time Period	Gain/Loss	# Winners	# Days	% Profitable	Benchmark Average	% Profitable Benchmark
NDX100	Most volume in 1 week		1 day	−0.01	453	838	54.06	0.05	54.05
NDX100	Most volume in 1 week		2 days	−0.01	411	837	49.1	0.1	53.03
NDX100	Most volume in 1 week		1 week	0.16	441	837	52.69	0.23	55.24
NDX100	Most volume in 1 month		1 day	−0.05	120	232	51.72	0.05	54.05
NDX100	Most volume in 1 month		2 days	−0.13	110	232	47.41	0.1	53.03
NDX100	Most volume in 1 month		1 week	0.45	124	232	53.45	0.23	55.24
NDX100	Most volume in 1 week, market rises today		1 day	−0.08	251	463	54.21	0.05	54.05
NDX100	Most volume in 1 week, market rises today		2 days	−0.19	224	463	48.38	0.1	53.03
NDX100	Most volume in 1 week, market rises today		1 week	0	239	463	51.62	0.23	55.24
NDX100	Most volume in 1 month, market rises today		1 day	−0.19	67	126	53.17	0.05	54.05
NDX100	Most volume in 1 month, market rises today		2 days	−0.3	62	126	49.21	0.1	53.03
NDX100	Most volume in 1 month, market rises today		1 week	0.43	71	126	56.35	0.23	55.24
NDX100	Most volume in 1 week, market falls today		1 day	0.1	202	373	54.16	0.05	54.05
NDX100	Most volume in 1 week, market falls today		2 days	0.25	187	372	50.27	0.1	53.03
NDX100	Most volume in 1 week, market falls today		1 week	0.38	202	372	54.3	0.23	55.24
NDX100	Most volume in 1 month, market falls today		1 day	0.15	53	105	50.48	0.05	54.05
NDX100	Most volume in 1 month, market falls today		2 days	0.12	48	105	45.71	0.1	53.03
NDX100	Most volume in 1 month, market falls today		1 week	0.53	53	105	50.48	0.23	55.24
NDX100	Most volume in 1 week, market rises today	Above 200-day MA	1 day	−0.02	180	322	55.9	0.06	55.39
NDX100	Most volume in 1 week, market rises today	Above 200-day MA	2 days	−0.01	165	322	51.24	0.14	54.61
NDX100	Most volume in 1 week, market rises today	Above 200-day MA	1 week	0.22	175	322	54.35	0.35	57.15

(continued)

TABLE 6.2 (*Continued*)

Index	Rule 1	Rule 2	Time Period	Gain/Loss	# Winners	# Days	% Profitable	Benchmark Average	Benchmark % Profitable Benchmark
NDX100	Most volume in 1 month, market rises today	Above 200-day MA	1 day	−0.21	52	96	54.17	0.06	55.39
NDX100	Most volume in 1 month, market rises today	Above 200-day MA	2 days	−0.28	48	96	50	0.14	54.61
NDX100	Most volume in 1 month, market rises today	Above 200-day MA	1 week	0.29	56	96	58.33	0.35	57.15
NDX100	Most volume in 1 week, market falls today	Above 200-day MA	1 day	0	130	233	55.79	0.06	55.39
NDX100	Most volume in 1 week, market falls today	Above 200-day MA	2 days	0.03	119	233	51.07	0.14	54.61
NDX100	Most volume in 1 week, market falls today	Above 200-day MA	1 week	0.23	127	233	54.51	0.35	57.15
NDX100	Most volume in 1 month, market falls today	Above 200-day MA	1 day	−0.02	35	66	53.03	0.06	55.39
NDX100	Most volume in 1 month, market falls today	Above 200-day MA	2 days	−0.35	29	66	43.94	0.14	54.61
NDX100	Most volume in 1 month, market falls today	Above 200-day MA	1 week	−0.12	32	66	48.48	0.35	57.15
NDX100	Most volume in 1 week, market rises today	Below 200-day MA	1 day	−0.24	71	141	50.35	0.02	51.26
NDX100	Most volume in 1 week, market rises today	Below 200-day MA	2 days	−0.62	59	141	41.84	0	49.76
NDX100	Most volume in 1 week, market rises today	Below 200-day MA	1 week	−0.49	64	141	45.39	−0.02	51.26
NDX100	Most volume in 1 month, market rises today	Below 200-day MA	1 day	−0.14	15	30	50	0.02	51.26
NDX100	Most volume in 1 month, market rises today	Below 200-day MA	2 days	−0.36	14	30	46.67	0	49.76
NDX100	Most volume in 1 month, market rises today	Below 200-day MA	1 week	0.89	15	30	50	−0.02	51.26
NDX100	Most volume in 1 week, market falls today	Below 200-day MA	1 day	0.26	72	140	51.43	0.02	51.26
NDX100	Most volume in 1 week, market falls today	Below 200-day MA	2 days	0.61	68	139	48.92	0	49.76
NDX100	Most volume in 1 week, market falls today	Below 200-day MA	1 week	0.63	75	139	53.96	−0.02	51.26
NDX100	Most volume in 1 month, market falls today	Below 200-day MA	1 day	0.44	18	39	46.15	0.02	51.26
NDX100	Most volume in 1 month, market falls today	Below 200-day MA	2 days	0.9	19	39	48.72	0	49.76
NDX100	Most volume in 1 month, market falls today	Below 200-day MA	1 week	1.63	21	39	53.85	−0.02	51.26

Summary and Conclusion

Is volume important? Based upon 22+ years of data, it is not.

In other chapters we used indicators or setups in a stand-alone fashion (as we did in this chapter) and in many of these cases an obvious edge existed. But, in looking at volume as a stand-alone indicator, there does not appear to be an obvious edge.

CHAPTER 7

Large Moves

Large one-day moves create a great deal of excitement. When prices rise sharply, you can feel the burst of energy it creates as analysts and financial market journalists excitedly tell us the good news as to why prices rose. And they usually go further by saying that today's big move up is likely to lead to a further rise in prices.

When prices drop significantly, the opposite is true. Bad economic news, poor earnings, and negative outlooks all become part of the nightly equation as to why prices dropped. And this negative psychology many times then tends to manifest itself in justifying why the outlook for the stock market is poor.

We looked at large moves in the S&P 500 (SPX) and the Nasdaq 100 (NDX) over a 22+-year period (January 1, 1989–September 30, 2011). For both markets, we looked at the days that rose or fell more than 1 percent and more than 2 percent (one should note, especially when looking at the time graphs, that the number of large daily moves increased in the late 1990s as volatility increased).

A sample of our findings is as follows.

Large Price Declines Outperform Large Price Gains

1. The most significant finding was that large declines in the SPX outperformed the average day by a healthy margin after one day, two days, and a week when the drop was 1 percent or more. When the drop was 2 percent or more, the performance jumped even more significantly.

Large Declines in the Nasdaq 100 Have Been Positive

2. Large declines in the NDX outperformed large rises.

Declines above the 200-Day Moving Average Were Significant

3. Two-percent drops for the SPX when above the 200-day moving average have led to significant large outperformance versus the benchmark. It also outperformed in the NDX for two days and a week.

See *Table Explanation* at the beginning of this book for column descriptions.

FIGURE 7.1 S&P 500: 1 percent Declines Have Outperformed 1 Percent Gains in the S&P 500 after One Week

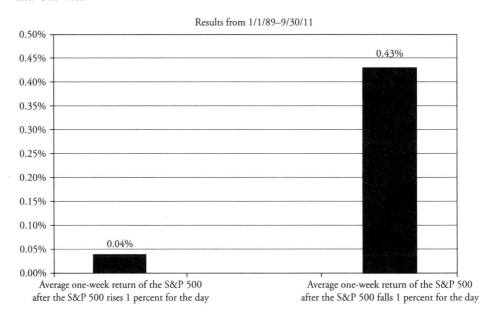

FIGURE 7.2 S&P 500: 2 Percent Declines Have Outperformed 2 Percent Gains in the S&P 500 after One Week

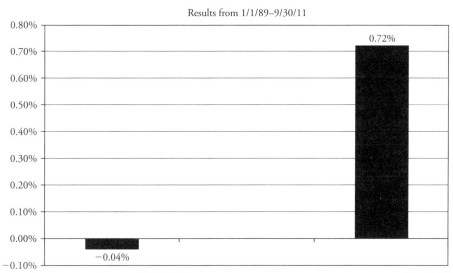

Results from 1/1/89–9/30/11

FIGURE 7.3 Nasdaq 100: 1 Percent Nasdaq Losses Have Outperformed 1 Percent Nasdaq Gains by a 5-1 Margin over One Week

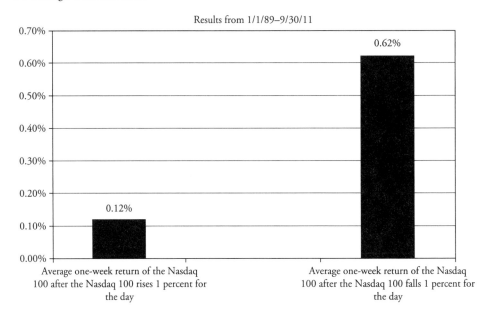

FIGURE 7.4 Nasdaq 100: 2 Percent Nasdaq Losses Have Outperformed 2 Percent Nasdaq Gains by a Significant Margin after One Week

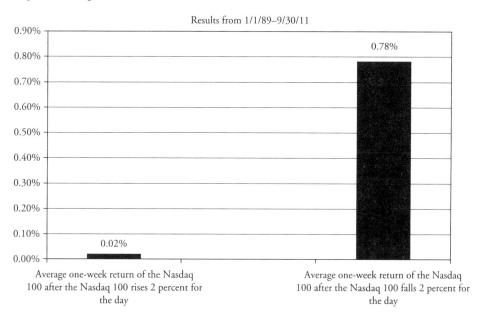

Results from 1/1/89–9/30/11

FIGURE 7.5 Time Graph Performance: S&P 500 Index Rises 1 Percent for the Day versus Falling
1 Percent for the Day

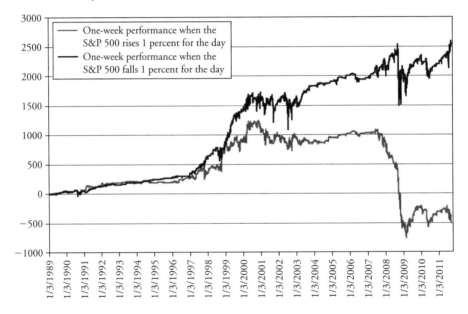

FIGURE 7.6 Time Graph Performance Comparison: Nasdaq 100 Index Rises 1 Percent for the Day versus Falling 1 Percent for the Day

TABLE 7.1 SPX Large Moves (1/1/1989 to 9/30/2011)

Index	Rule 1	Rule 2	Time Period	Gain/Loss	# Winners	# Days	% Profitable	Benchmark Average	% Profitable Benchmark
SP500	Rises 1%		1 day	0.03	393	776	50.64	0.03	53.43
SP500	Rises 1%		2 days	−0.01	411	776	52.96	0.06	53.92
SP500	Rises 1%		1 week	0.04	416	774	53.75	0.15	56.19
SP500	Rises 2%		1 day	−0.04	99	197	50.25	0.03	53.43
SP500	Rises 2%		2 days	−0.18	104	197	52.79	0.06	53.92
SP500	Rises 2%		1 week	−0.04	114	196	58.16	0.15	56.19
SP500	Falls 1%		1 day	0.15	415	737	56.31	0.03	53.43
SP500	Falls 1%		2 days	0.24	400	737	54.27	0.06	53.92
SP500	Falls 1%		1 week	0.43	419	736	56.93	0.15	56.19
SP500	Falls 2%		1 day	0.29	128	213	60.09	0.03	53.43
SP500	Falls 2%		2 days	0.43	118	213	55.4	0.06	53.92
SP500	Falls 2%		1 week	0.72	122	212	57.55	0.15	56.19
SP500	Rises 1%	Above 200-day MA	1 day	0.05	241	468	51.5	0.04	54.12
SP500	Rises 1%	Above 200-day MA	2 days	0.1	263	468	56.2	0.08	55.29
SP500	Rises 1%	Above 200-day MA	1 week	0.18	256	468	54.7	0.19	57.22
SP500	Rises 2%	Above 200-day MA	1 day	0.09	35	69	50.72	0.04	54.12
SP500	Rises 2%	Above 200-day MA	2 days	0.22	42	69	60.87	0.08	55.29
SP500	Rises 2%	Above 200-day MA	1 week	0.46	43	69	62.32	0.19	57.22
SP500	Falls 1%	Above 200-day MA	1 day	0.13	190	322	59.01	0.04	54.12
SP500	Falls 1%	Above 200-day MA	2 days	0.16	178	322	55.28	0.08	55.29
SP500	Falls 1%	Above 200-day MA	1 week	0.47	186	322	57.76	0.19	57.22

SP500	Falls 2%	Above 200-day MA	1 day	0.32	37	55	67.27	0.04	54.12
SP500	Falls 2%	Above 200-day MA	2 days	0.39	33	55	60	0.08	55.29
SP500	Falls 2%	Above 200-day MA	1 week	0.65	28	55	50.91	0.19	57.22
SP500	Rises 1%	Below 200-day MA	1 day	0	152	308	49.35	0.01	51.7
SP500	Rises 1%	Below 200-day MA	2 days	−0.18	148	308	48.05	0.02	50.52
SP500	Rises 1%	Below 200-day MA	1 week	−0.16	160	306	52.29	0.06	53.6
SP500	Rises 2%	Below 200-day MA	1 day	−0.1	64	128	50	0.01	51.7
SP500	Rises 2%	Below 200-day MA	2 days	−0.39	62	128	48.44	0.02	50.52
SP500	Rises 2%	Below 200-day MA	1 week	−0.32	71	127	55.91	0.06	53.6
SP500	Falls 1%	Below 200-day MA	1 day	0.16	225	415	54.22	0.01	51.7
SP500	Falls 1%	Below 200-day MA	2 days	0.3	222	415	53.49	0.02	50.52
SP500	Falls 1%	Below 200-day MA	1 week	0.4	233	414	56.28	0.06	53.6
SP500	Falls 2%	Below 200-day MA	1 day	0.28	91	158	57.59	0.01	51.7
SP500	Falls 2%	Below 200-day MA	2 days	0.44	85	158	53.8	0.02	50.52
SP500	Falls 2%	Below 200-day MA	1 week	0.75	94	157	59.87	0.06	53.6

TABLE 7.2 NDX Large Moves (1/1/1989 to 9/30/2011)

Index	Rule 1	Rule 2	Time Period	Gain/Loss	# Winners	# Days	% Profitable	Benchmark Average	% Profitable Benchmark
NDX100	Rises 1%		1 day	0.02	735	1361	54	0.06	54.26
NDX100	Rises 1%		2 days	−0.02	713	1361	52.39	0.12	53.54
NDX100	Rises 1%		1 week	0.12	761	1360	55.96	0.29	56.17
NDX100	Rises 2%		1 day	−0.03	298	564	52.84	0.06	54.26
NDX100	Rises 2%		2 days	−0.18	293	564	51.95	0.12	53.54
NDX100	Rises 2%		1 week	0.02	308	564	54.61	0.29	56.17
NDX100	Falls 1%		1 day	0.11	671	1244	53.94	0.06	54.26
NDX100	Falls 1%		2 days	0.31	675	1243	54.3	0.12	53.54
NDX100	Falls 1%		1 week	0.62	706	1242	56.84	0.29	56.17
NDX100	Falls 2%		1 day	0.24	313	566	55.3	0.06	54.26
NDX100	Falls 2%		2 days	0.51	319	566	56.36	0.12	53.54
NDX100	Falls 2%		1 week	0.78	326	566	57.6	0.29	56.17
NDX100	Rises 1%	Above 200-day MA	1 day	0.07	528	954	55.35	0.07	54.97
NDX100	Rises 1%	Above 200-day MA	2 days	0.12	517	954	54.19	0.14	54.62
NDX100	Rises 1%	Above 200-day MA	1 week	0.39	563	954	59.01	0.36	57.34
NDX100	Rises 2%	Above 200-day MA	1 day	0.03	182	333	54.65	0.07	54.97
NDX100	Rises 2%	Above 200-day MA	2 days	0.12	184	333	55.26	0.14	54.62
NDX100	Rises 2%	Above 200-day MA	1 week	0.53	198	333	59.46	0.36	57.34
NDX100	Falls 1%	Above 200-day MA	1 day	0.07	391	708	55.23	0.07	54.97
NDX100	Falls 1%	Above 200-day MA	2 days	0.24	395	708	55.79	0.14	54.62
NDX100	Falls 1%	Above 200-day MA	1 week	0.57	401	708	56.64	0.36	57.34

NDX100	Falls 2%	Above 200-day MA	1 day	0.27	148	248	59.68	0.07	54.97
NDX100	Falls 2%	Above 200-day MA	2 days	0.42	148	248	59.68	0.14	54.62
NDX100	Falls 2%	Above 200-day MA	1 week	0.88	144	248	58.06	0.36	57.34
NDX100	Rises 1%	Below 200-day MA	1 day	−0.08	207	407	50.86	0.04	52.52
NDX100	Rises 1%	Below 200-day MA	2 days	−0.35	196	407	48.16	0.06	50.85
NDX100	Rises 1%	Below 200-day MA	1 week	−0.51	198	406	48.77	0.14	53.26
NDX100	Rises 2%	Below 200-day MA	1 day	−0.11	116	231	50.22	0.04	52.52
NDX100	Rises 2%	Below 200-day MA	2 days	−0.6	109	231	47.19	0.06	50.85
NDX100	Rises 2%	Below 200-day MA	1 week	−0.71	110	231	47.62	0.14	53.26
NDX100	Falls 1%	Below 200-day MA	1 day	0.16	280	536	52.24	0.04	52.52
NDX100	Falls 1%	Below 200-day MA	2 days	0.41	280	535	52.34	0.06	50.85
NDX100	Falls 1%	Below 200-day MA	1 week	0.68	305	534	57.12	0.14	53.26
NDX100	Falls 2%	Below 200-day MA	1 day	0.21	165	318	51.89	0.04	52.52
NDX100	Falls 2%	Below 200-day MA	2 days	0.59	171	318	53.77	0.06	50.85
NDX100	Falls 2%	Below 200-day MA	1 week	0.71	182	318	57.23	0.14	53.26

Summary and Conclusion

Large market drops are often followed by immediate snap back moves. This is especially true during the times when the S&P 500 has traded above its 200-day moving average. After panic has set in and the selling is finished, the market many times has quickly recovered, and these recoveries are often strong.

Now let's see how the market has done when an abundance of stocks were making new 52-week highs or 52-week lows.

CHAPTER 8

New 52-Week Highs, New 52-Week Lows

It is widely assumed that the more stocks making new 52-week highs, the healthier the market is, and this healthy condition is often a prelude to further upward movement. And it's also widely assumed that the more stocks making new 52-week lows, the weaker the market condition is and the weaker the outlook is for stocks. These assumptions appear to be wrong.

We used the HILO Index for looking at these assumptions. The HILO Index is a daily number that subtracts the number of new 52-week lows for the day from the number of new 52-week highs for the day (new 52-week highs minus new 52-week lows). The higher the number, the more stocks made new highs versus new lows. A negative number means that more stocks made new 52-week lows for the day than 52-week highs.

We looked at the data from January 1, 1993 through September 30, 2011 for the S&P 500 (SPX) and from September 20, 1995 through September 30, 2011 for the Nasdaq 100 (NDX). We looked at the HILO Index, making a new 1-week high (low), a new 5-week high (low), and a new 10-week high (low). What we found was that 1-week lows, 5-week lows, and 10-week lows of the HILO Index outperform 1-, 5-, and 10-week highs over a 1-week and 2-week period. These findings are consistent with many of the findings in other chapters that show it's been better to be a buyer on short-term weakness versus being a buyer after market strength has occurred.

See *Table Explanation* at the beginning of this book for column descriptions.

FIGURE 8.1   S&P 500: One-Week Lows in the HILO Index Have Outperformed One-Week Highs in the HILO Index

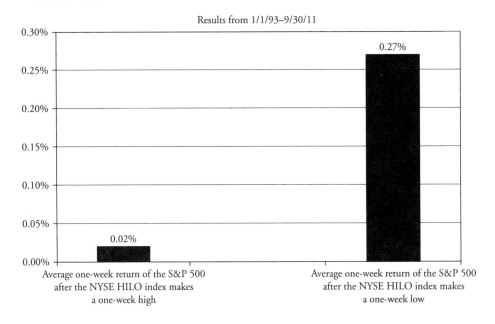

FIGURE 8.2   S&P 500: Five-Week Lows in the HILO Index Have Led to Greater Returns than Five-Week Highs in the Index

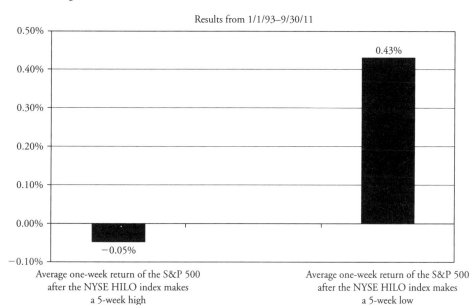

FIGURE 8.3 Nasdaq 100: The Nasdaq Has Seen Gains of Better than 2:1 after the HILO Index Made a New One-Week Low versus a New One-Week High

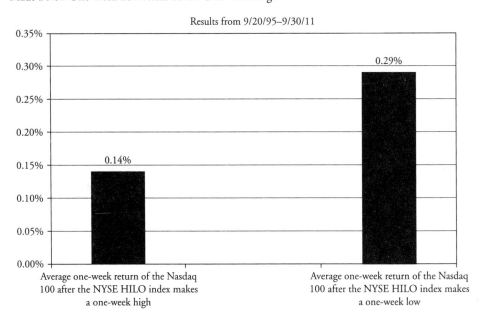

FIGURE 8.4 Time Graph Performance Comparison: S&P 500 Index after the HILO Index Makes a One-Week High versus a One-Week Low

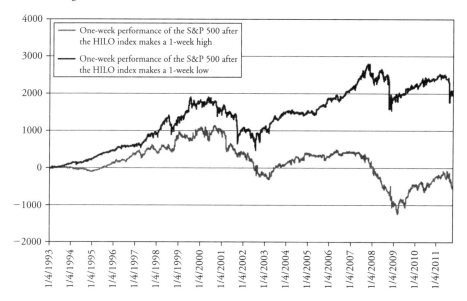

FIGURE 8.5 Time Graph Performance Comparison: Nasdaq 100 Index after the HILO Index Makes a One-Week High versus a One-Week Low

TABLE 8.1 SPX 52-Week Highs and 52-Week Lows (1/1/1993 to 9/30/2011)

Index	Rule 1	Rule 2	Time Period	Gain/Loss	# Winners	# Days	% Profitable	Benchmark Average	% Profitable Benchmark
SP500	1-wk high of NYSEHILO		1 week	0.02	661	1236	53.48	0.14	56.03
SP500	1-wk high of NYSEHILO		2 weeks	0.11	700	1236	56.63	0.27	57.91
SP500	5-wk high of NYSEHILO		1 week	−0.05	184	348	52.87	0.14	56.03
SP500	5-wk high of NYSEHILO		2 weeks	−0.04	197	348	56.61	0.27	57.91
SP500	10-wk high of NYSEHILO		1 week	0.02	115	214	53.74	0.14	56.03
SP500	10-wk high of NYSEHILO		2 weeks	0.06	122	214	57.01	0.27	57.91
SP500	1-wk low of NYSEHILO		1 week	0.27	685	1184	57.85	0.14	56.03
SP500	1-wk low of NYSEHILO		2 weeks	0.38	708	1181	59.95	0.27	57.91
SP500	5-wk low of NYSEHILO		1 week	0.43	204	364	56.04	0.14	56.03
SP500	5-wk low of NYSEHILO		2 weeks	0.37	208	363	57.3	0.27	57.91
SP500	10-wk low of NYSEHILO		1 week	0.29	121	231	52.38	0.14	56.03
SP500	10-wk low of NYSEHILO		2 weeks	0.28	125	231	54.11	0.27	57.91
SP500	1-wk high of NYSEHILO	Above 200-day MA	1 week	0.11	484	879	55.06	0.19	57.42
SP500	1-wk high of NYSEHILO	Above 200-day MA	2 weeks	0.3	527	879	59.95	0.4	60.01
SP500	5-wk high of NYSEHILO	Above 200-day MA	1 week	0.17	151	269	56.13	0.19	57.42
SP500	5-wk high of NYSEHILO	Above 200-day MA	2 weeks	0.28	167	269	62.08	0.4	60.01
SP500	10-wk high of NYSEHILO	Above 200-day MA	1 week	0.16	97	173	56.07	0.19	57.42
SP500	10-wk high of NYSEHILO	Above 200-day MA	2 weeks	0.26	107	173	61.85	0.4	60.01
SP500	1-wk low of NYSEHILO	Above 200-day MA	1 week	0.29	466	784	59.44	0.19	57.42
SP500	1-wk low of NYSEHILO	Above 200-day MA	2 weeks	0.43	480	784	61.22	0.4	60.01
SP500	5-wk low of NYSEHILO	Above 200-day MA	1 week	0.3	126	217	58.06	0.19	57.42

(continued)

TABLE 8.1 (*Continued*)

Index	Rule 1	Rule 2	Time Period	Gain/Loss	# Winners	# Days	% Profitable	Benchmark Average	% Profitable Benchmark
SP500	5-wk low of NYSEHILO	Above 200-day MA	2 weeks	0.32	127	217	58.53	0.4	60.01
SP500	10-wk low of NYSEHILO	Above 200-day MA	1 week	0.15	72	134	53.73	0.19	57.42
SP500	10-wk low of NYSEHILO	Above 200-day MA	2 weeks	0.07	72	134	53.73	0.4	60.01
SP500	1-wk high of NYSEHILO	Below 200-day MA	1 week	−0.19	177	357	49.58	0.02	52.83
SP500	1-wk high of NYSEHILO	Below 200-day MA	2 weeks	−0.37	173	357	48.46	−0.03	53.09
SP500	5-wk high of NYSEHILO	Below 200-day MA	1 week	−0.81	33	79	41.77	0.02	52.83
SP500	5-wk high of NYSEHILO	Below 200-day MA	2 weeks	−1.12	30	79	37.97	−0.03	53.09
SP500	10-wk high of NYSEHILO	Below 200-day MA	1 week	−0.56	18	41	43.9	0.02	52.83
SP500	10-wk high of NYSEHILO	Below 200-day MA	2 weeks	−0.8	15	41	36.59	−0.03	53.09
SP500	1-wk low of NYSEHILO	Below 200-day MA	1 week	0.22	219	400	54.75	0.02	52.83
SP500	1-wk low of NYSEHILO	Below 200-day MA	2 weeks	0.29	228	397	57.43	−0.03	53.09
SP500	5-wk low of NYSEHILO	Below 200-day MA	1 week	0.62	78	147	53.06	0.02	52.83
SP500	5-wk low of NYSEHILO	Below 200-day MA	2 weeks	0.45	81	146	55.48	−0.03	53.09
SP500	10-wk low of NYSEHILO	Below 200-day MA	1 week	0.48	49	97	50.52	0.02	52.83
SP500	10-wk low of NYSEHILO	Below 200-day MA	2 weeks	0.55	53	97	54.64	−0.03	53.09

TABLE 8.2 NDX 52-Week Highs and 52-Week Lows (9/20/1995 to 9/30/2011)

Index	Rule 1	Rule 2	Time Period	Gain/Loss	# Winners	# Days	% Profitable	Benchmark Average	% Profitable Benchmark
NDX100	1-wk high of NYSEHILO		1 week	0.14	583	1064	54.79	0.27	55.58
NDX100	1-wk high of NYSEHILO		2 weeks	0.31	604	1064	56.77	0.53	56.94
NDX100	5-wk high of NYSEHILO		1 week	0.18	174	335	51.94	0.27	55.58
NDX100	5-wk high of NYSEHILO		2 weeks	0.42	192	335	57.31	0.53	56.94
NDX100	10-wk high of NYSEHILO		1 week	0.11	113	217	52.07	0.27	55.58
NDX100	10-wk high of NYSEHILO		2 weeks	0.43	122	217	56.22	0.53	56.94
NDX100	1-wk low of NYSEHILO		1 week	0.29	537	992	54.13	0.27	55.58
NDX100	1-wk low of NYSEHILO		2 weeks	0.6	567	989	57.33	0.53	56.94
NDX100	5-wk low of NYSEHILO		1 week	0.22	169	340	49.71	0.27	55.58
NDX100	5-wk low of NYSEHILO		2 weeks	0.14	162	339	47.79	0.53	56.94
NDX100	10-wk low of NYSEHILO		1 week	0.18	107	210	50.95	0.27	55.58
NDX100	10-wk low of NYSEHILO		2 weeks	−0.34	97	210	46.19	0.53	56.94
NDX100	1-wk high of NYSEHILO	Above 200-day MA	1 week	0.27	436	762	57.22	0.36	56.79
NDX100	1-wk high of NYSEHILO	Above 200-day MA	2 weeks	0.66	446	762	58.53	0.75	58.51
NDX100	5-wk high of NYSEHILO	Above 200-day MA	1 week	0.17	136	252	53.97	0.36	56.79
NDX100	5-wk high of NYSEHILO	Above 200-day MA	2 weeks	0.43	139	252	55.16	0.75	58.51
NDX100	10-wk high of NYSEHILO	Above 200-day MA	1 week	0.19	93	174	53.45	0.36	56.79
NDX100	10-wk high of NYSEHILO	Above 200-day MA	2 weeks	0.77	100	174	57.47	0.75	58.51
NDX100	1-wk low of NYSEHILO	Above 200-day MA	1 week	0.32	348	638	54.55	0.36	56.79
NDX100	1-wk low of NYSEHILO	Above 200-day MA	2 weeks	0.9	390	637	61.22	0.75	58.51
NDX100	5-wk low of NYSEHILO	Above 200-day MA	1 week	0.04	93	197	47.21	0.36	56.79

(*continued*)

TABLE 8.2 (Continued)

Index	Rule 1	Rule 2	Time Period	Gain/Loss	# Winners	# Days	% Profitable	Benchmark Average	% Profitable Benchmark
NDX100	5-wk low of NYSEHILO	Above 200-day MA	2 weeks	0.42	99	197	50.25	0.75	58.51
NDX100	10-wk low of NYSEHILO	Above 200-day MA	1 week	0.07	60	118	50.85	0.36	56.79
NDX100	10-wk low of NYSEHILO	Above 200-day MA	2 weeks	0.09	59	118	50	0.75	58.51
NDX100	1-wk high of NYSEHILO	Below 200-day MA	1 week	−0.18	147	302	48.68	0.06	52.57
NDX100	1-wk high of NYSEHILO	Below 200-day MA	2 weeks	−0.57	158	302	52.32	−0.02	52.98
NDX100	5-wk high of NYSEHILO	Below 200-day MA	1 week	0.23	38	83	45.78	0.06	52.57
NDX100	5-wk high of NYSEHILO	Below 200-day MA	2 weeks	0.39	53	83	63.86	−0.02	52.98
NDX100	10-wk high of NYSEHILO	Below 200-day MA	1 week	−0.21	20	43	46.51	0.06	52.57
NDX100	10-wk high of NYSEHILO	Below 200-day MA	2 weeks	−0.94	22	43	51.16	−0.02	52.98
NDX100	1-wk low of NYSEHILO	Below 200-day MA	1 week	0.25	189	354	53.39	0.06	52.57
NDX100	1-wk low of NYSEHILO	Below 200-day MA	2 weeks	0.06	177	352	50.28	−0.02	52.98
NDX100	5-wk low of NYSEHILO	Below 200-day MA	1 week	0.47	76	143	53.15	0.06	52.57
NDX100	5-wk low of NYSEHILO	Below 200-day MA	2 weeks	−0.25	63	142	44.37	−0.02	52.98
NDX100	10-wk low of NYSEHILO	Below 200-day MA	1 week	0.33	47	92	51.09	0.06	52.57
NDX100	10-wk low of NYSEHILO	Below 200-day MA	2 weeks	−0.89	38	92	41.3	−0.02	52.98

Summary and Conclusion

A market making a number of new 52-week highs is usually viewed as bullish, and a market making a number of new 52-week lows is usually viewed as bearish. Over the longer term, this may or may not be true, but when looking at prices over a short-term period, there has been no edge in viewing the market this way.

Now let's move to two popular sentiment indicators: the put/call ratio and the volatility index.

CHAPTER 9

Put/Call Ratio

We now look at the put/call ratio, an indicator that is widely used by market professionals.

The put/call ratio is the total number of puts divided by the total number of calls for all index and equity options traded on the Chicago Board of Options Exchange (CBOE). It is widely assumed that the put/call ratio acts as a contrary indicator. High readings (meaning an abundance of put buying versus call buying) supposedly means that there is much fear in the marketplace and that a reversal is likely near. Low readings (lots of call buying or little put buying) means there is complacency and confidence in the marketplace.

We looked at two scenarios (all scenarios used closing data).

A summary of our tests is as follows:

Our first scenario looked at when the 1-month moving average of the ratio made a new 20-day high and a new 20-day low. We used the 1-month average because (for some unknown reason) it has become commonly relied upon in trading circles.

A summary of our findings follows.

Twenty-Day High Put/Call Ratio Moving Averages Showed Some Edges

1. We found small edges in this approach, especially compared to the benchmark over a one-week period of time.

   The second scenario we looked at was when the put/call ratio made either a 5-day high, a 10-day high, a 5-day low, or a 10-day low. Our findings showed the following.

Short-Term Lows on the Put/Call Ratio Are Followed by Market Underperformance

1. The 5-day lows and the 10-day lows both underperformed or equaled the benchmark. In fact, the 10-day lows lost money after a week in both the S&P 500 and the Nasdaq 100. This is good information for profit taking, waiting for long entries, and for potential short selling.
2. There does not seem to be much of an edge when the ratio made a 5-day high or a 10-day high.

See *Table Explanation* at the beginning of this book for column descriptions.

FIGURE 9.1   Time Graph Performance Comparison: S&P 500 Index after the Put/Call Ratio Makes a 5-Day High versus a 5-Day Low

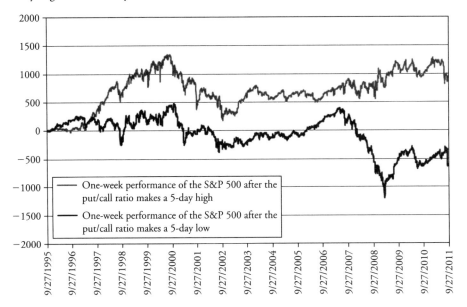

FIGURE 9.2 Time Graph Performance Comparison: Nasdaq 100 Index after the Put/Call Ratio Makes a 5-Day High versus a 5-Day Low

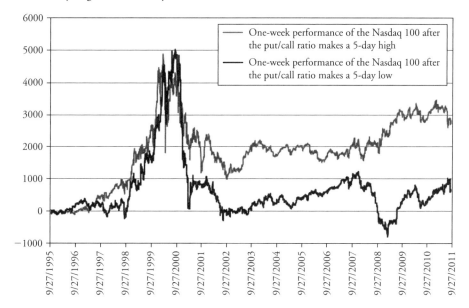

TABLE 9.1 SPX Put/Call Ratios (9/27/1995 to 9/30/2011)

Index	Rule 1	Rule 2	Time Period	Gain/Loss	# Winners	# Days	% Profitable	Benchmark Average	% Profitable Benchmark
SP500	P/C 21-day MA makes a 20-day high		1 day	0.08	429	789	54.37	0.03	53.15
SP500	P/C 21-day MA makes a 20-day high		2 days	0.13	435	789	55.13	0.05	53.73
SP500	P/C 21-day MA makes a 20-day high		1 week	0.27	449	789	56.91	0.12	55.26
SP500	P/C 21-day MA makes a 20-day low		1 day	0.01	428	817	52.39	0.03	53.15
SP500	P/C 21-day MA makes a 20-day low		2 days	−0.02	424	817	51.9	0.05	53.73
SP500	P/C 21-day MA makes a 20-day low		1 week	0.15	475	817	58.14	0.12	55.26
SP500	P/C 21-day MA makes a 20-day high	Above 200-day MA	1 day	0.1	269	476	56.51	0.04	54.21
SP500	P/C 21-day MA makes a 20-day high	Above 200-day MA	2 days	0.17	279	476	58.61	0.08	55.61
SP500	P/C 21-day MA makes a 20-day high	Above 200-day MA	1 week	0.36	282	476	59.24	0.18	56.9
SP500	P/C 21-day MA makes a 20-day low	Above 200-day MA	1 day	0	312	599	52.09	0.04	54.21
SP500	P/C 21-day MA makes a 20-day low	Above 200-day MA	2 days	0.02	317	599	52.92	0.08	55.61
SP500	P/C 21-day MA makes a 20-day low	Above 200-day MA	1 week	0.21	359	599	59.93	0.18	56.9
SP500	P/C 21-day MA makes a 20-day high	Below 200-day MA	1 day	0.06	160	313	51.12	0	50.95
SP500	P/C 21-day MA makes a 20-day high	Below 200-day MA	2 days	0.06	156	313	49.84	0	49.85
SP500	P/C 21-day MA makes a 20-day high	Below 200-day MA	1 week	0.14	167	313	53.35	−0.01	51.87
SP500	P/C 21-day MA makes a 20-day low	Below 200-day MA	1 day	0.04	116	218	53.21	0	50.95
SP500	P/C 21-day MA makes a 20-day low	Below 200-day MA	2 days	−0.1	107	218	49.08	0	49.85
SP500	P/C 21-day MA makes a 20-day low	Below 200-day MA	1 week	−0.03	116	218	53.21	−0.01	51.87
SP500	P/C closes at a 5-day high		1 day	−0.01	476	900	52.89	0.03	53.15
SP500	P/C closes at a 5-day high		2 days	0.03	477	900	53	0.05	53.73
SP500	P/C closes at a 5-day high		1 week	0.15	494	899	54.95	0.12	55.26

SP500	P/C closes at a 10-day high		1 day	−0.02	263	510	51.57	0.03	53.15
SP500	P/C closes at a 10-day high		2 days	−0.01	268	510	52.55	0.05	53.73
SP500	P/C closes at a 10-day high		1 week	0	264	509	51.87	0.12	55.26
SP500	P/C closes at a 5-day low		1 day	0.07	512	918	55.77	0.03	53.15
SP500	P/C closes at a 5-day low		2 days	−0.01	492	918	53.59	0.05	53.73
SP500	P/C closes at a 5-day low		1 week	−0.01	499	917	54.42	0.12	55.26
SP500	P/C closes at a 10-day low		1 day	−0.02	270	503	53.68	0.03	53.15
SP500	P/C closes at a 10-day low		2 days	−0.18	260	503	51.69	0.05	53.73
SP500	P/C closes at a 10-day low		1 week	−0.29	252	503	50.1	0.12	55.26
SP500	P/C closes at a 5-day high	Above 200-day MA	1 day	0.03	334	601	55.57	0.04	54.21
SP500	P/C closes at a 5-day high	Above 200-day MA	2 days	0.05	332	601	55.24	0.08	55.61
SP500	P/C closes at a 5-day high	Above 200-day MA	1 week	0.17	334	601	55.57	0.18	56.9
SP500	P/C closes at a 10-day high	Above 200-day MA	1 day	0.08	190	335	56.72	0.04	54.21
SP500	P/C closes at a 10-day high	Above 200-day MA	2 days	0.11	190	335	56.72	0.08	55.61
SP500	P/C closes at a 10-day high	Above 200-day MA	1 week	0.09	177	335	52.84	0.18	56.9
SP500	P/C closes at a 5-day low	Above 200-day MA	1 day	0.08	355	630	56.35	0.04	54.21
SP500	P/C closes at a 5-day low	Above 200-day MA	2 days	0.06	348	630	55.24	0.08	55.61
SP500	P/C closes at a 5-day low	Above 200-day MA	1 week	0.08	349	630	55.4	0.18	56.9
SP500	P/C closes at a 10-day low	Above 200-day MA	1 day	0	184	342	53.8	0.04	54.21
SP500	P/C closes at a 10-day low	Above 200-day MA	2 days	−0.08	182	342	53.22	0.08	55.61
SP500	P/C closes at a 10-day low	Above 200-day MA	1 week	−0.15	174	342	50.88	0.18	56.9
SP500	P/C closes at a 5-day high	Below 200-day MA	1 day	−0.1	142	299	47.49	0	50.95
SP500	P/C closes at a 5-day high	Below 200-day MA	2 days	−0.01	145	299	48.5	0	49.85

(continued)

TABLE 9.1 (*Continued*)

Index	Rule 1	Rule 2	Time Period	Gain/Loss	# Winners	# Days	% Profitable	Benchmark Average	% Profitable Benchmark
SP500	P/C closes at a 5-day high	Below 200-day MA	1 week	0.1	160	298	53.69	−0.01	51.87
SP500	P/C closes at a 10-day high	Below 200-day MA	1 day	−0.2	73	175	41.71	0	50.95
SP500	P/C closes at a 10-day high	Below 200-day MA	2 days	−0.24	78	175	44.57	0	49.85
SP500	P/C closes at a 10-day high	Below 200-day MA	1 week	−0.19	87	174	50	−0.01	51.87
SP500	P/C closes at a 5-day low	Below 200-day MA	1 day	0.04	157	288	54.51	0	50.95
SP500	P/C closes at a 5-day low	Below 200-day MA	2 days	−0.15	144	288	50	0	49.85
SP500	P/C closes at a 5-day low	Below 200-day MA	1 week	−0.21	150	287	52.26	−0.01	51.87
SP500	P/C closes at a 10-day low	Below 200-day MA	1 day	−0.08	86	161	53.42	0	50.95
SP500	P/C closes at a 10-day low	Below 200-day MA	2 days	−0.41	78	161	48.45	0	49.85
SP500	P/C closes at a 10-day low	Below 200-day MA	1 week	−0.59	78	161	48.45	−0.01	51.87

122

TABLE 9.2 NDX Put/Call Ratios (9/27/1995 to 9/30/2011)

Index	Rule 1	Rule 2	Time Period	Gain/Loss	# Winners	# Days	% Profitable	Benchmark Average	% Profitable Benchmark
NDX100	P/C 21-day MA makes a 20-day high		1 day	0.14	425	789	53.87	0.05	53.89
NDX100	P/C 21-day MA makes a 20-day high		2 days	0.2	414	789	52.47	0.1	53.19
NDX100	P/C 21-day MA makes a 20-day high		1 week	0.47	450	789	57.03	0.25	55.16
NDX100	P/C 21-day MA makes a 20-day low		1 day	0.02	439	817	53.73	0.05	53.89
NDX100	P/C 21-day MA makes a 20-day low		2 days	0.02	433	817	53	0.1	53.19
NDX100	P/C 21-day MA makes a 20-day low		1 week	0.35	484	817	59.24	0.25	55.16
NDX100	P/C 21-day MA makes a 20-day high	Above 200-day MA	1 day	0.11	266	485	54.85	0.06	54.94
NDX100	P/C 21-day MA makes a 20-day high	Above 200-day MA	2 days	0.2	261	485	53.81	0.14	54.55
NDX100	P/C 21-day MA makes a 20-day high	Above 200-day MA	1 week	0.7	281	485	57.94	0.36	56.77
NDX100	P/C 21-day MA makes a 20-day low	Above 200-day MA	1 day	0.05	341	617	55.27	0.06	54.94
NDX100	P/C 21-day MA makes a 20-day low	Above 200-day MA	2 days	0.14	342	617	55.43	0.14	54.55
NDX100	P/C 21-day MA makes a 20-day low	Above 200-day MA	1 week	0.55	385	617	62.4	0.36	56.77
NDX100	P/C 21-day MA makes a 20-day high	Below 200-day MA	1 day	0.19	159	304	52.3	0.03	51.53
NDX100	P/C 21-day MA makes a 20-day high	Below 200-day MA	2 days	0.2	153	304	50.33	0.03	50.12
NDX100	P/C 21-day MA makes a 20-day high	Below 200-day MA	1 week	0.1	169	304	55.59	0.01	51.54
NDX100	P/C 21-day MA makes a 20-day low	Below 200-day MA	1 day	−0.09	98	200	49	0.03	51.53
NDX100	P/C 21-day MA makes a 20-day low	Below 200-day MA	2 days	−0.35	91	200	45.5	0.03	50.12
NDX100	P/C 21-day MA makes a 20-day low	Below 200-day MA	1 week	−0.26	99	200	49.5	0.01	51.54
NDX100	P/C closes at a 5-day high		1 day	0.05	498	900	55.33	0.05	53.89
NDX100	P/C closes at a 5-day high		2 days	0.12	457	900	50.78	0.1	53.19
NDX100	P/C closes at a 5-day high		1 week	0.3	482	899	53.62	0.25	55.16

(continued)

123

TABLE 9.2 (*Continued*)

Index	Rule 1	Rule 2	Time Period	Gain/Loss	# Winners	# Days	% Profitable	Benchmark Average	% Profitable Benchmark
NDX100	P/C closes at a 10-day high		1 day	0.04	275	510	53.92	0.05	53.89
NDX100	P/C closes at a 10-day high		2 days	0.07	258	510	50.59	0.1	53.19
NDX100	P/C closes at a 10-day high		1 week	0.17	265	509	52.06	0.25	55.16
NDX100	P/C closes at a 5-day low		1 day	0.08	506	918	55.12	0.05	53.89
NDX100	P/C closes at a 5-day low		2 days	−0.01	473	918	51.53	0.1	53.19
NDX100	P/C closes at a 5-day low		1 week	0.11	499	917	54.42	0.25	55.16
NDX100	P/C closes at a 10-day low		1 day	−0.06	251	503	49.9	0.05	53.89
NDX100	P/C closes at a 10-day low		2 days	−0.29	253	503	50.3	0.1	53.19
NDX100	P/C closes at a 10-day low		1 week	−0.35	248	503	49.3	0.25	55.16
NDX100	P/C closes at a 5-day high	Above 200-day MA	1 day	0.03	346	618	55.99	0.06	54.94
NDX100	P/C closes at a 5-day high	Above 200-day MA	2 days	0.13	320	618	51.78	0.14	54.55
NDX100	P/C closes at a 5-day high	Above 200-day MA	1 week	0.26	329	618	53.24	0.36	56.77
NDX100	P/C closes at a 10-day high	Above 200-day MA	1 day	0.12	190	338	56.21	0.06	54.94
NDX100	P/C closes at a 10-day high	Above 200-day MA	2 days	0.26	184	338	54.44	0.14	54.55
NDX100	P/C closes at a 10-day high	Above 200-day MA	1 week	0.31	175	338	51.78	0.36	56.77
NDX100	P/C closes at a 5-day low	Above 200-day MA	1 day	0.14	369	652	56.6	0.06	54.94
NDX100	P/C closes at a 5-day low	Above 200-day MA	2 days	0.13	347	652	53.22	0.14	54.55
NDX100	P/C closes at a 5-day low	Above 200-day MA	1 week	0.38	373	652	57.21	0.36	56.77
NDX100	P/C closes at a 10-day low	Above 200-day MA	1 day	0.04	182	351	51.85	0.06	54.94
NDX100	P/C closes at a 10-day low	Above 200-day MA	2 days	−0.03	190	351	54.13	0.14	54.55
NDX100	P/C closes at a 10-day low	Above 200-day MA	1 week	0.03	189	351	53.85	0.36	56.77

NDX100	P/C closes at a 5-day high	Below 200-day MA	1 day	0.1	152	282	53.9	0.03	51.53
NDX100	P/C closes at a 5-day high	Below 200-day MA	2 days	0.11	137	282	48.58	0.03	50.12
NDX100	P/C closes at a 5-day high	Below 200-day MA	1 week	0.41	153	281	54.45	0.01	51.54
NDX100	P/C closes at a 10-day high	Below 200-day MA	1 day	−0.12	85	172	49.42	0.03	51.53
NDX100	P/C closes at a 10-day high	Below 200-day MA	2 days	−0.3	74	172	43.02	0.03	50.12
NDX100	P/C closes at a 10-day high	Below 200-day MA	1 week	−0.1	90	171	52.63	0.01	51.54
NDX100	P/C closes at a 5-day low	Below 200-day MA	1 day	−0.07	137	266	51.5	0.03	51.53
NDX100	P/C closes at a 5-day low	Below 200-day MA	2 days	−0.38	126	266	47.37	0.03	50.12
NDX100	P/C closes at a 5-day low	Below 200-day MA	1 week	−0.55	126	265	47.55	0.01	51.54
NDX100	P/C closes at a 10-day low	Below 200-day MA	1 day	−0.29	69	152	45.39	0.03	51.53
NDX100	P/C closes at a 10-day low	Below 200-day MA	2 days	−0.88	63	152	41.45	0.03	50.12
NDX100	P/C closes at a 10-day low	Below 200-day MA	1 week	−1.22	59	152	38.82	0.01	51.54

Conclusion and Summary

Even though the put/call ratio is popular and quoted often, there have not been extremely large historical edges using the ratio. After we initially published these results in 2004, a number of professional options traders contacted us and stated the same thing.

There are two main points here. The first just because an indicator is widely quoted that doesn't mean it works.

The second point is that there are better indicators related to options than the put/call ratio. You'll see this in the next chapter on the volatility index.

CHAPTER 10

Volatility Index (VIX)

The CBOE Volatility Index (VIX) is a measurement of the implied volatility of the S&P 500 options. The VIX measures market sentiment and is used by professional traders to gauge the amount of fear and complacency in the marketplace. High VIX readings are usually accompanied by a market that has recently declined, and low VIX reading are usually accompanied by a market that has recently risen.

There are a number of ways to use the VIX but before we go into that, we first need to mention how *not* to use it. Over the past decade, many people have used "static" numbers with the VIX. The common theme for many years was to sell the market when the VIX reached the low 20s level and buy the market when it reached 30. Unfortunately, that turned out to be a recipe for disaster (as every other static reading analysis on the VIX has been). In the summer of 2002 the VIX not only crossed 30 and triggered the supposedly magical buy signal, but it proceeded to rise to above 50 over the next few months. The S&P 500 (SPX) dropped significantly as this buy signal was in place. And then, in late 2003, the VIX went into the low 20s again triggering a magical signal (this time sell), yet the market proceeded to rally and the VIX headed into the teens, leaving these short sellers with substantial losses. *If there is one truism that we've found, it is the fact that static numbers do not work when it comes to the VIX.*

Now, let's look at our tests and see if the VIX can be used to help you time your market entries. We looked at a period from 1990 (the first available calculations from the Chicago Board Options Exchange (CBOE) for the VIX) through September 30, 2011 (20+ years). We looked at the VIX as it stretched beyond its 10-day moving average. We used this average to keep the measurement dynamic versus using a static number. This means we are constantly looking at the VIX and comparing it to where it has been on average over the past 10 days versus today.

A summary of the findings is as follows.

When the VIX Has Closed 10 Percent or More Above Its 10-Period Moving Average, the Market Has Outperformed the Average Gains

1. The further the VIX rises above its 10-period moving average, the greater the likelihood that the market will move higher and the greater the likelihood that

this market reversal to the upside will be greater than the average daily move of a normal market. We can see this when the VIX closes 5 percent above its moving average, 10 percent above its moving average, and especially 15 percent above its moving average. The edge is fairly consistent over a 1-day period, a 2-day period, and a 1-week period. In fact the 1-week gain in the SPX when the VIX is 10 percent above its 10-day moving average is more than *triple* the average weekly gain over the 20+-year period.

The VIX Closing 5 Percent or More below Its 10-Period Moving Average Has Seen the Market Lose Money over the Next Week

2. When the VIX closes more than 5 percent below its 10-period moving average, the market has greatly underperformed the averages. In fact, in all cases the market lost money over the short term. This finding is extremely significant because it identifies the times when the least amount of money has been made over the past 20+ years. For example, over the 20+-year period, the VIX has closed 5 percent under its 10-period moving average approximately 1,432 trading days. The SPX rose over 220 percent over this 20+-year period but none of the cumulative net weekly gains have occurred while the VIX closed 5 percent under its 10-period moving average. *This information confirms that the VIX can identify overbought markets and helps you identify the times that you should be aggressive in locking in gains and/or avoiding long purchases.*

The Nasdaq Behavior Has Approximately Mirrored the S&P 500 Behavior When the VIX Has Been Stretched

3. We looked at the VXN, which is the Nasdaq version of the VIX from February 1, 2001, to September 30, 2011, to see how the Nasdaq performed when the VIX closed above and below its 10-period moving average. It was interesting to see how the results carried over into the Nasdaq. The Nasdaq's average daily, 2-day, and 1-week gain improved when the VIX was 5 percent and 10 percent above its moving average. And the Nasdaq significantly underperformed when the VIX closed 5 percent and 10 percent below its moving average. These findings further confirm the significance of the VIX in guiding you when to enter the market, when not to enter the market, and when to be more aggressive in locking in both long and short gains.

See *Table Explanation* at the beginning of this book for column descriptions.

FIGURE 10.1   S&P 500: The Market on Average Has Lost Money within a Week When the VIX Has Closed at Least 5 Percent below Its 10-Period Moving Average

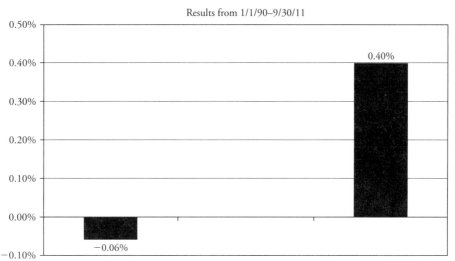

Average one-week return of the S&P 500 after the VIX closes at least 5 percent below its 10-day moving average

Average one-week return of the S&P 500 after the VIX closes at least 5 percent above its 10-day moving average

FIGURE 10.2 S&P 500: The Market Has Outperformed During the Times the VIX Has Closed 10 Percent or More above Its 10-Period Moving Average; the Opposite Is True When It Has Closed 10 Percent or More below Its 10-Period Moving Average

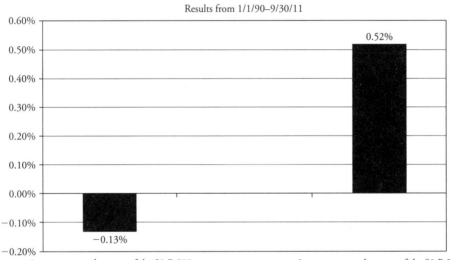

Results from 1/1/90–9/30/11

Average one-week return of the S&P 500 after the VIX closes at least 10 percent below its 10-day moving average

Average one-week return of the S&P 500 after the VIX closes at least 10 percent above its 10-day moving average

FIGURE 10.3 S&P 500: 15 Percent VIX Stretches below the 10-Period Moving Average Have Been Followed by Strong Market Gains

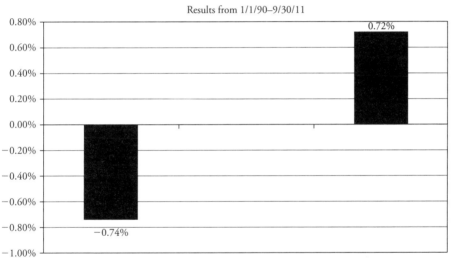

Results from 1/1/90–9/30/11

0.72%

−0.74%

Average one-week return of the S&P 500 after the VIX closes at least 15 percent below its 10-day moving average

Average one-week return of the S&P 500 after the VIX closes at least 15 percent above its 10-day moving average

FIGURE 10.4 Nasdaq 100: The Nasdaq Has Shown a Stronger Gain over One Week When the VXN Has Closed 5 Percent above Its 10-Period Moving Average versus 5 Percent Below

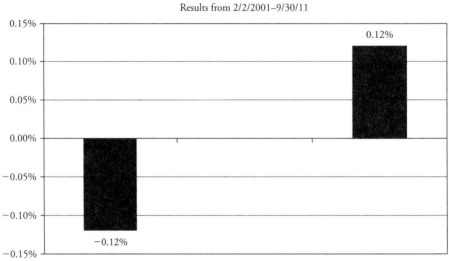

Results from 2/2/2001–9/30/11

Average one-week return of the Nasdaq 100 after the VXN closes at least 5 percent below its 10-day moving average

Average one-week return of the Nasdaq 100 after the VXN closes at least 5 percent above its 10-day moving average

FIGURE 10.5 Nasdaq 100: 10 Percent VXN Stretches above Its 10-Period Moving Average Have Outperformed 10 Percent VXN Stretches below Its 10-Period Moving Average

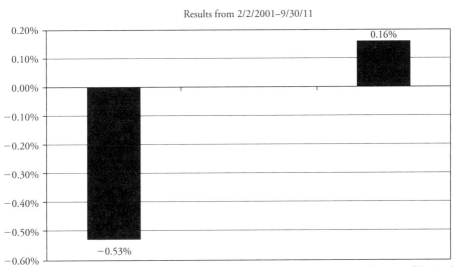

Results from 2/2/2001–9/30/11

FIGURE 10.6   Nasdaq 100: When the VXN Has Closed 15 Percent above Its 10-Period Moving Average, the Nasdaq Has Proceeded to Rally Strongly over the Next Week

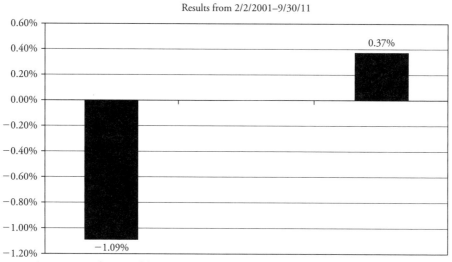

Results from 2/2/2001–9/30/11

Average one-week return of the Nasdaq 100 after the VXN closes at least 15 percent below its 10-day moving average

Average one-week return of the Nasdaq 100 after the VXN closes at least 15 percent above its 10-day moving average

FIGURE 10.7   Time Graph Performance Comparison: S&P 500 Index When the VIX Closes at Least 5 Percent below Its 10-Day Moving Average versus at Least 5 Percent above Its 10-Day Moving Average

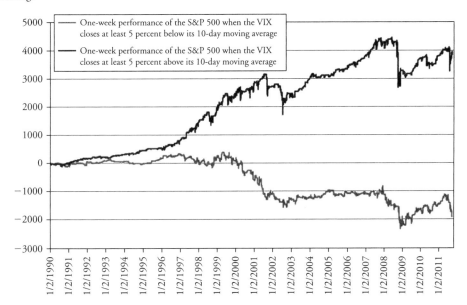

FIGURE 10.8   Time Graph Performance Comparison: S&P 500 Index When the VIX Closes at Least 10 Percent below Its 10-Day Moving Average versus at Least 10 Percent above Its 10-Day Moving Average

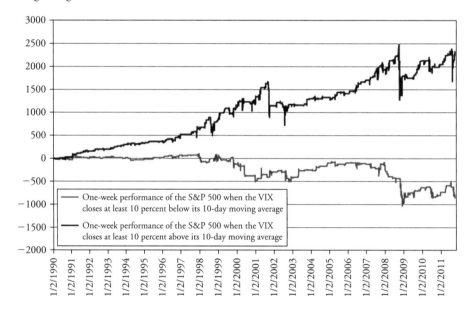

FIGURE 10.9 Time Graph Performance Comparison: Nasdaq 100 Index When the VXN Closes at Least 5 Percent below Its 10-Day Moving Average versus at Least 5 Percent above Its 10-Day Moving Average

FIGURE 10.10 Time Graph Performance Comparison: Nasdaq 100 Index When the VXN Closes at Least 10 Percent below Its 10-Day Moving Average versus at Least 10 Percent above Its 10-Day Moving Average

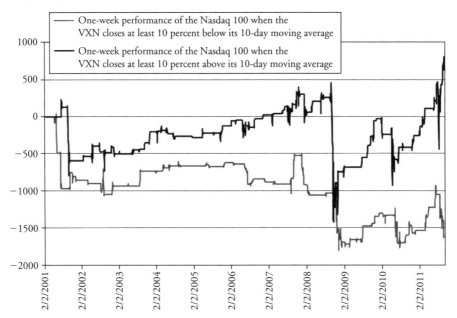

TABLE 10.1 SPX Volatility Index (VIX: 1/2/1990 to 9/30/2011)

Index	Rule 1	Rule 2	Time Period	Gain/Loss	# Winners	# Days	% Profitable	Benchmark Average	% Profitable Benchmark
SP500	Within 2%		1 day	0.04	632	1152	54.86	0.03	53.13
SP500	Within 2%		2 days	0.06	614	1152	53.3	0.06	53.7
SP500	Within 2%		1 week	0.13	634	1152	55.03	0.14	55.69
SP500	5% above		1 day	0.12	689	1242	55.48	0.03	53.13
SP500	5% above		2 days	0.18	698	1242	56.2	0.06	53.7
SP500	5% above		1 week	0.4	731	1240	58.95	0.14	55.69
SP500	10% above		1 day	0.16	317	562	56.41	0.03	53.13
SP500	10% above		2 days	0.26	328	562	58.36	0.06	53.7
SP500	10% above		1 week	0.52	340	561	60.61	0.14	55.69
SP500	15% above		1 day	0.38	154	250	61.6	0.03	53.13
SP500	15% above		2 days	0.54	158	250	63.2	0.06	53.7
SP500	15% above		1 week	0.72	160	250	64	0.14	55.69
SP500	5% below		1 day	−0.02	720	1432	50.28	0.03	53.13
SP500	5% below		2 days	−0.04	750	1432	52.37	0.06	53.7
SP500	5% below		1 week	−0.06	763	1432	53.28	0.14	55.69
SP500	10% below		1 day	−0.02	216	416	51.92	0.03	53.13
SP500	10% below		2 days	−0.16	213	416	51.2	0.06	53.7
SP500	10% below		1 week	−0.13	213	416	51.2	0.14	55.69
SP500	15% below		1 day	−0.21	43	90	47.78	0.03	53.13
SP500	15% below		2 days	−0.55	39	90	43.33	0.06	53.7
SP500	15% below		1 week	−0.74	38	90	42.22	0.14	55.69

(*continued*)

139

TABLE 10.1 (*Continued*)

Index	Rule 1	Rule 2	Time Period	Gain/Loss	# Winners	# Days	% Profitable	Benchmark Average	% Profitable Benchmark
SP500	Within 2%	Above 200-day MA	1 day	0.03	470	851	55.23	0.03	53.74
SP500	Within 2%	Above 200-day MA	2 days	0.04	454	851	53.35	0.07	55.07
SP500	Within 2%	Above 200-day MA	1 week	0.14	467	851	54.88	0.17	56.58
SP500	5% above	Above 200-day MA	1 day	0.11	440	768	57.29	0.03	53.74
SP500	5% above	Above 200-day MA	2 days	0.2	448	768	58.33	0.07	55.07
SP500	5% above	Above 200-day MA	1 week	0.48	475	768	61.85	0.17	56.58
SP500	10% above	Above 200-day MA	1 day	0.09	178	297	59.93	0.03	53.74
SP500	10% above	Above 200-day MA	2 days	0.24	184	297	61.95	0.07	55.07
SP500	10% above	Above 200-day MA	1 week	0.52	186	297	62.63	0.17	56.58
SP500	15% above	Above 200-day MA	1 day	0.33	78	123	63.41	0.03	53.74
SP500	15% above	Above 200-day MA	2 days	0.4	77	123	62.6	0.07	55.07
SP500	15% above	Above 200-day MA	1 week	0.67	84	123	68.29	0.17	56.58
SP500	5% below	Above 200-day MA	1 day	0.01	503	988	50.91	0.03	53.74
SP500	5% below	Above 200-day MA	2 days	0.02	532	988	53.85	0.07	55.07
SP500	5% below	Above 200-day MA	1 week	0.01	534	988	54.05	0.17	56.58
SP500	10% below	Above 200-day MA	1 day	0.05	136	265	51.32	0.03	53.74
SP500	10% below	Above 200-day MA	2 days	−0.01	140	265	52.83	0.07	55.07
SP500	10% below	Above 200-day MA	1 week	−0.1	134	265	50.57	0.17	56.58
SP500	15% below	Above 200-day MA	1 day	−0.02	18	45	40	0.03	53.74
SP500	15% below	Above 200-day MA	2 days	−0.17	20	45	44.44	0.07	55.07
SP500	15% below	Above 200-day MA	1 week	−0.46	20	45	44.44	0.17	56.58

SP500	Within 2%	Below 200-day MA	1 day	0.07	162	301	53.82	0.01	51.7
SP500	Within 2%	Below 200-day MA	2 days	0.13	160	301	53.16	0.02	50.52
SP500	Within 2%	Below 200-day MA	1 week	0.09	167	301	55.48	0.06	53.6
SP500	5% above	Below 200-day MA	1 day	0.12	249	474	52.53	0.01	51.7
SP500	5% above	Below 200-day MA	2 days	0.15	250	474	52.74	0.02	50.52
SP500	5% above	Below 200-day MA	1 week	0.27	256	472	54.24	0.06	53.6
SP500	10% above	Below 200-day MA	1 day	0.24	139	265	52.45	0.01	51.7
SP500	10% above	Below 200-day MA	2 days	0.29	144	265	54.34	0.02	50.52
SP500	10% above	Below 200-day MA	1 week	0.53	154	264	58.33	0.06	53.6
SP500	15% above	Below 200-day MA	1 day	0.42	76	127	59.84	0.01	51.7
SP500	15% above	Below 200-day MA	2 days	0.68	81	127	63.78	0.02	50.52
SP500	15% above	Below 200-day MA	1 week	0.77	76	127	59.84	0.06	53.6
SP500	5% below	Below 200-day MA	1 day	−0.09	217	444	48.87	0.01	51.7
SP500	5% below	Below 200-day MA	2 days	−0.18	218	444	49.1	0.02	50.52
SP500	5% below	Below 200-day MA	1 week	−0.21	229	444	51.58	0.06	53.6
SP500	10% below	Below 200-day MA	1 day	−0.14	80	151	52.98	0.01	51.7
SP500	10% below	Below 200-day MA	2 days	−0.41	73	151	48.34	0.02	50.52
SP500	10% below	Below 200-day MA	1 week	−0.19	79	151	52.32	0.06	53.6
SP500	15% below	Below 200-day MA	1 day	−0.41	25	45	55.56	0.01	51.7
SP500	15% below	Below 200-day MA	2 days	−0.94	19	45	42.22	0.02	50.52
SP500	15% below	Below 200-day MA	1 week	−1.02	18	45	40	0.06	53.6

TABLE 10.2 NDX Volatility Index (VXN: 2/2/2001 to 9/30/2011)

Index	Rule 1	Rule 2	Time Period	Gain/Loss	# Winners	# Days	% Profitable	Benchmark Average	% Profitable Benchmark
NDX100	Within 2%		1 day	−0.06	315	614	51.3	0.01	53.56
NDX100	Within 2%		2 days	−0.02	309	614	50.33	0.02	52.31
NDX100	Within 2%		1 week	0.08	320	614	52.12	0.06	53.64
NDX100	5% above		1 day	0.12	317	558	56.81	0.01	53.56
NDX100	5% above		2 days	0.15	302	557	54.22	0.02	52.31
NDX100	5% above		1 week	0.12	310	554	55.96	0.06	53.64
NDX100	10% above		1 day	0.21	134	241	55.6	0.01	53.56
NDX100	10% above		2 days	0.23	127	240	52.92	0.02	52.31
NDX100	10% above		1 week	0.16	134	238	56.3	0.06	53.64
NDX100	15% above		1 day	0.14	53	101	52.48	0.01	53.56
NDX100	15% above		2 days	0.28	55	101	54.46	0.02	52.31
NDX100	15% above		1 week	0.37	57	101	56.44	0.06	53.64
NDX100	5% below		1 day	−0.11	339	645	52.56	0.01	53.56
NDX100	5% below		2 days	−0.17	339	645	52.56	0.02	52.31
NDX100	5% below		1 week	−0.12	346	645	53.64	0.06	53.64
NDX100	10% below		1 day	−0.06	88	161	54.66	0.01	53.56
NDX100	10% below		2 days	−0.2	84	161	52.17	0.02	52.31
NDX100	10% below		1 week	−0.53	76	161	47.21	0.06	53.64
NDX100	15% below		1 day	−0.37	18	33	54.55	0.01	53.56
NDX100	15% below		2 days	−0.99	16	33	48.48	0.02	52.31
NDX100	15% below		1 week	−1.09	12	33	36.36	0.06	53.64

NDX100	Within 2%	Above 200-day MA	1 day	−0.02	203	387	52.45	0.02	54.8
NDX100	Within 2%	Above 200-day MA	2 days	−0.02	203	387	52.45	0.05	54.23
NDX100	Within 2%	Above 200-day MA	1 week	−0.02	202	387	52.2	0.13	55.36
NDX100	5% above	Above 200-day MA	1 day	0.05	163	284	57.39	0.02	54.8
NDX100	5% above	Above 200-day MA	2 days	0.15	159	284	55.99	0.05	54.23
NDX100	5% above	Above 200-day MA	1 week	0.38	168	284	59.15	0.13	55.36
NDX100	10% above	Above 200-day MA	1 day	0.07	70	120	58.33	0.02	54.8
NDX100	10% above	Above 200-day MA	2 days	0.06	60	120	50	0.05	54.23
NDX100	10% above	Above 200-day MA	1 week	0.44	69	120	57.5	0.13	55.36
NDX100	15% above	Above 200-day MA	1 day	0.18	31	51	60.78	0.02	54.8
NDX100	15% above	Above 200-day MA	2 days	0.26	29	51	56.86	0.05	54.23
NDX100	15% above	Above 200-day MA	1 week	0.27	29	51	56.86	0.13	55.36
NDX100	5% below	Above 200-day MA	1 day	0.03	223	397	56.17	0.02	54.8
NDX100	5% below	Above 200-day MA	2 days	0.09	225	397	56.68	0.05	54.23
NDX100	5% below	Above 200-day MA	1 week	0.25	232	397	58.44	0.13	55.36
NDX100	10% below	Above 200-day MA	1 day	0.15	58	90	64.44	0.02	54.8
NDX100	10% below	Above 200-day MA	2 days	0.28	54	90	60	0.05	54.23
NDX100	10% below	Above 200-day MA	1 week	0.45	54	90	60	0.13	55.36
NDX100	15% below	Above 200-day MA	1 day	−0.02	14	21	66.67	0.02	54.8
NDX100	15% below	Above 200-day MA	2 days	−0.35	12	21	57.14	0.05	54.23
NDX100	15% below	Above 200-day MA	1 week	−0.25	10	21	47.62	0.13	55.36
NDX100	Within 2%	Below 200-day MA	1 day	−0.13	112	227	49.34	0	51.75
NDX100	Within 2%	Below 200-day MA	2 days	−0.01	106	227	46.7	−0.02	49.49
NDX100	Within 2%	Below 200-day MA	1 week	0.26	118	227	51.98	−0.05	51.11

(continued)

TABLE 10.2 (*Continued*)

Index	Rule 1	Rule 2	Time Period	Gain/Loss	# Winners	# Days	% Profitable	Benchmark Average	% Profitable Benchmark
NDX100	5% above	Below 200-day MA	1 day	0.19	154	274	56.2	0	51.75
NDX100	5% above	Below 200-day MA	2 days	0.15	143	273	52.38	−0.02	49.49
NDX100	5% above	Below 200-day MA	1 week	−0.15	142	270	52.59	−0.05	51.11
NDX100	10% above	Below 200-day MA	1 day	0.36	64	121	52.89	0	51.75
NDX100	10% above	Below 200-day MA	2 days	0.41	67	120	55.83	−0.02	49.49
NDX100	10% above	Below 200-day MA	1 week	−0.11	65	118	55.08	−0.05	51.11
NDX100	15% above	Below 200-day MA	1 day	0.1	22	50	44	0	51.75
NDX100	15% above	Below 200-day MA	2 days	0.29	26	50	52	−0.02	49.49
NDX100	15% above	Below 200-day MA	1 week	0.46	28	50	56	−0.05	51.11
NDX100	5% below	Below 200-day MA	1 day	−0.34	116	248	46.77	0	51.75
NDX100	5% below	Below 200-day MA	2 days	−0.58	114	248	45.97	−0.02	49.49
NDX100	5% below	Below 200-day MA	1 week	−0.71	114	248	45.97	−0.05	51.11
NDX100	10% below	Below 200-day MA	1 day	−0.31	30	71	42.25	0	51.75
NDX100	10% below	Below 200-day MA	2 days	−0.81	30	71	42.25	−0.02	49.49
NDX100	10% below	Below 200-day MA	1 week	−1.77	22	71	30.99	−0.05	51.11
NDX100	15% below	Below 200-day MA	1 day	−1	4	12	33.33	0	51.75
NDX100	15% below	Below 200-day MA	2 days	−2.12	4	12	33.33	−0.02	49.49
NDX100	15% below	Below 200-day MA	1 week	−2.56	2	12	16.67	−0.05	51.11

Summary and Conclusion

In summary, the VIX acts as a barometer to guide you as to how aggressive you should be on the long side, short side, locking in long gains, and locking in short gains. As the VIX moves further above its moving average, the likelihood of a market rally increases. The opposite is true when it moves further below its 10-period moving average. These findings have been fairly consistent and steady for the past 20+ years.

As you can see especially from the first time graph, simply being out of the market when the VIX closes 5 percent or more below its 10-period moving average has significantly improved a static buy-and-hold strategy for the S&P 500 index.

CHAPTER 11

The Two-Period RSI Indicator

The historical edges in this chapter are the largest in this book.

In 2003 we began publishing research on the 2-period Relative Strength Index (RSI). Up until that time, most, if not all, of the research which was available on RSI was specifically on the 14-period RSI, which was the original setting used by Welles Wilder, the creator of the indicator in the 1970s.

We tested the original 14-period RSI extensively and could not find any statistical evidence that edges existed in using it. As we started shortening the time frame, though, we saw that it showed a short-term predictive ability, especially when the RSI period was lowered and its levels reached extremes.

The following are the test results for the past two decades using the 2-period RSI at extreme levels. What you will see is strong evidence that since 1989, this indicator has done an excellent job of predicting short-term movement in the major indices.

1. Low RSI levels (especially below 2) have led to significant outperformance in the S&P. The average gains per trade and the percentage correct are the highest in this book.
2. High RSI levels have ultimately led to dead money as rallies have often stalled within a few days.
3. Extreme low RSI levels below the 200-day have seen healthy short-term gains. We've seen these extremely oversold, dead-cat bounces in other indicators and in this one especially.
4. The Nasdaq has seen a larger than normal gain on both sides of the extremes with the greatest edges coming when the RSI is at its lowest levels.

Let's now look at the statistics.

See *Table Explanation* at the beginning of this book for column descriptions.

FIGURE 11.1 S&P 500: When the 2-Period RSI Has Been under 5 in the S&P 500 It Has Outperformed Compared to When the 2-Period RSI Has Been above 95

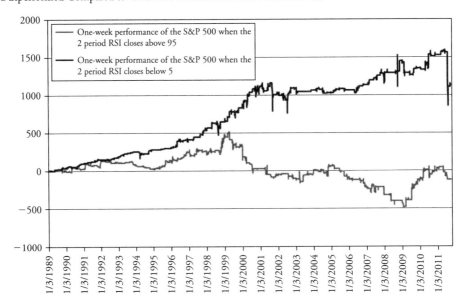

FIGURE 11.2 Nasdaq 100: Also, When the 2-Period RSI Has Been under 5 in the Nasdaq 100 It Has Outperformed Compared to When the 2-Period RSI Has Been above 95

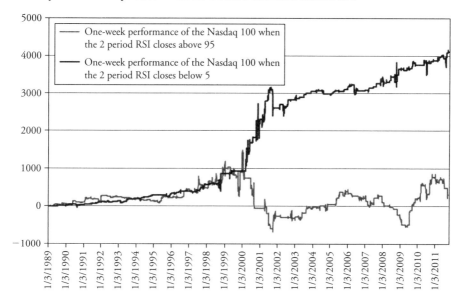

TABLE 11.1 SPX Two-Period RSI Study (1/1/1989 to 9/30/2011)

Index	Rule 1	Rule 2	Time Period	Gain/Loss	# Winners	# Days	% Profitable	Benchmark Average	% Profitable Benchmark
SP500	RSI2 > 99		1 day	0.06	39	82	47.56	0.03	53.43
SP500	RSI2 > 99		2 days	0.07	44	82	53.66	0.06	53.92
SP500	RSI2 > 99		1 week	0.08	50	82	60.98	0.15	56.19
SP500	RSI2 > 98		1 day	0.02	84	174	48.28	0.03	53.43
SP500	RSI2 > 98		2 days	−0.01	87	174	50	0.06	53.92
SP500	RSI2 > 98		1 week	0.13	103	174	59.2	0.15	56.19
SP500	RSI2 > 95		1 day	−0.03	221	481	45.95	0.03	53.43
SP500	RSI2 > 95		2 days	−0.03	243	481	50.52	0.06	53.92
SP500	RSI2 > 95		1 week	0.09	271	481	56.34	0.15	56.19
SP500	RSI2 < 1		1 day	1.41	27	35	77.14	0.03	53.43
SP500	RSI2 < 1		2 days	1.72	30	35	85.71	0.06	53.92
SP500	RSI2 < 1		1 week	1.75	24	35	68.57	0.15	56.19
SP500	RSI2 < 2		1 day	0.64	63	89	70.79	0.03	53.43
SP500	RSI2 < 2		2 days	0.94	65	89	73.03	0.06	53.92
SP500	RSI2 < 2		1 week	1.16	60	89	67.42	0.15	56.19
SP500	RSI2 < 5		1 day	0.29	186	297	62.63	0.03	53.43
SP500	RSI2 < 5		2 days	0.44	189	297	63.64	0.06	53.92
SP500	RSI2 < 5		1 week	0.58	179	297	60.27	0.15	56.19
SP500	RSI2 > 99	Above 200-day MA	1 day	0.06	38	79	48.1	0.04	54.12
SP500	RSI2 > 99	Above 200-day MA	2 days	0.09	42	79	53.16	0.08	55.29
SP500	RSI2 > 99	Above 200-day MA	1 week	0.14	50	79	63.29	0.19	57.22

SP500	RSI2 > 98	Above 200-day MA	1 day	0.03	78	159	49.06	0.04	54.12
SP500	RSI2 > 98	Above 200-day MA	2 days	0.01	79	159	49.69	0.08	55.29
SP500	RSI2 > 98	Above 200-day MA	1 week	0.18	96	159	60.38	0.19	57.22
SP500	RSI2 > 95	Above 200-day MA	1 day	0	194	421	46.08	0.04	54.12
SP500	RSI2 > 95	Above 200-day MA	2 days	0.01	215	421	51.07	0.08	55.29
SP500	RSI2 > 95	Above 200-day MA	1 week	0.12	238	421	56.53	0.19	57.22
SP500	RSI2 < 1	Above 200-day MA	1 day	0.49	6	8	75	0.04	54.12
SP500	RSI2 < 1	Above 200-day MA	2 days	0.73	8	8	100	0.08	55.29
SP500	RSI2 < 1	Above 200-day MA	1 week	1.43	7	8	87.5	0.19	57.22
SP500	RSI2 < 2	Above 200-day MA	1 day	0.51	26	34	76.47	0.04	54.12
SP500	RSI2 < 2	Above 200-day MA	2 days	0.85	26	34	76.47	0.08	55.29
SP500	RSI2 < 2	Above 200-day MA	1 week	1.15	26	34	76.47	0.19	57.22
SP500	RSI2 < 5	Above 200-day MA	1 day	0.34	96	143	67.13	0.04	54.12
SP500	RSI2 < 5	Above 200-day MA	2 days	0.62	98	143	68.53	0.08	55.29
SP500	RSI2 < 5	Above 200-day MA	1 week	0.68	97	143	67.83	0.19	57.22
SP500	RSI2 > 99	Below 200-day MA	1 day	0.17	1	3	33.33	0.01	51.7
SP500	RSI2 > 99	Below 200-day MA	2 days	−0.55	2	3	66.67	0.02	50.52
SP500	RSI2 > 99	Below 200-day MA	1 week	−1.56	0	3	0	0.06	53.6
SP500	RSI2 > 98	Below 200-day MA	1 day	−0.09	6	15	40	0.01	51.7
SP500	RSI2 > 98	Below 200-day MA	2 days	−0.22	8	15	53.33	0.02	50.52
SP500	RSI2 > 98	Below 200-day MA	1 week	−0.36	7	15	46.67	0.06	53.6
SP500	RSI2 > 95	Below 200-day MA	1 day	−0.19	27	60	45	0.01	51.7
SP500	RSI2 > 95	Below 200-day MA	2 days	−0.33	28	60	46.67	0.02	50.52
SP500	RSI2 > 95	Below 200-day MA	1 week	−0.14	33	60	55	0.06	53.6

(continued)

TABLE 11.1 (*Continued*)

Index	Rule 1	Rule 2	Time Period	Gain/Loss	# Winners	# Days	% Profitable	Benchmark Average	% Profitable Benchmark
SP500	RSI2 < 1	Below 200-day MA	1 day	1.68	21	27	77.78	0.01	51.7
SP500	RSI2 < 1	Below 200-day MA	2 days	2.01	22	27	81.48	0.02	50.52
SP500	RSI2 < 1	Below 200-day MA	1 week	1.85	17	27	62.96	0.06	53.6
SP500	RSI2 < 2	Below 200-day MA	1 day	0.72	37	55	67.27	0.01	51.7
SP500	RSI2 < 2	Below 200-day MA	2 days	1	39	55	70.91	0.02	50.52
SP500	RSI2 < 2	Below 200-day MA	1 week	1.17	34	55	61.82	0.06	53.6
SP500	RSI2 < 5	Below 200-day MA	1 day	0.24	90	154	58.44	0.01	51.7
SP500	RSI2 < 5	Below 200-day MA	2 days	0.28	91	154	59.09	0.02	50.52
SP500	RSI2 < 5	Below 200-day MA	1 week	0.49	82	154	53.25	0.06	53.6

TABLE 11.2 NDX Two-Period RSI Study (1/1/1989 to 9/30/2011)

Index	Rule 1	Rule 2	Time Period	Gain/Loss	# Winners	# Days	% Profitable	Benchmark Average	% Profitable Benchmark
NDX100	RSI2 > 99		1 day	0.13	102	170	60	0.06	54.26
NDX100	RSI2 > 99		2 days	0.28	98	170	57.65	0.12	53.54
NDX100	RSI2 > 99		1 week	0.86	120	170	70.59	0.29	56.17
NDX100	RSI2 > 98		1 day	0.1	168	288	58.33	0.06	54.26
NDX100	RSI2 > 98		2 days	0.18	165	288	57.29	0.12	53.54
NDX100	RSI2 > 98		1 week	0.57	183	288	63.54	0.29	56.17
NDX100	RSI2 > 95		1 day	0.04	330	582	56.7	0.06	54.26
NDX100	RSI2 > 95		2 days	0.08	327	582	56.19	0.12	53.54
NDX100	RSI2 > 95		1 week	0.32	336	582	57.73	0.29	56.17
NDX100	RSI2 < 1		1 day	0.45	29	51	56.86	0.06	54.26
NDX100	RSI2 < 1		2 days	1.22	36	51	70.59	0.12	53.54
NDX100	RSI2 < 1		1 week	1.25	31	51	60.78	0.29	56.17
NDX100	RSI2 < 2		1 day	0.59	62	110	56.36	0.06	54.26
NDX100	RSI2 < 2		2 days	1.08	70	110	63.64	0.12	53.54
NDX100	RSI2 < 2		1 week	1.09	69	110	62.73	0.29	56.17
NDX100	RSI2 < 5		1 day	0.52	178	307	57.98	0.06	54.26
NDX100	RSI2 < 5		2 days	0.74	188	307	61.24	0.12	53.54
NDX100	RSI2 < 5		1 week	1.11	199	307	64.82	0.29	56.17
NDX100	RSI2 > 99	Above 200-day MA	1 day	0.13	94	159	59.12	0.07	54.97
NDX100	RSI2 > 99	Above 200-day MA	2 days	0.23	90	159	56.6	0.14	54.62
NDX100	RSI2 > 99	Above 200-day MA	1 week	0.76	111	159	69.81	0.36	57.34

(continued)

TABLE 11.2 (Continued)

Index	Rule 1	Rule 2	Time Period	Gain/Loss	# Winners	# Days	% Profitable	Benchmark Average	% Profitable Benchmark
NDX100	RSI2 > 98	Above 200-day MA	1 day	0.15	156	265	58.87	0.07	54.97
NDX100	RSI2 > 98	Above 200-day MA	2 days	0.27	154	265	58.11	0.14	54.62
NDX100	RSI2 > 98	Above 200-day MA	1 week	0.66	170	265	64.15	0.36	57.34
NDX100	RSI2 > 95	Above 200-day MA	1 day	0.09	290	505	57.43	0.07	54.97
NDX100	RSI2 > 95	Above 200-day MA	2 days	0.18	292	505	57.82	0.14	54.62
NDX100	RSI2 > 95	Above 200-day MA	1 week	0.41	301	505	59.6	0.36	57.34
NDX100	RSI2 < 1	Above 200-day MA	1 day	0.03	5	8	62.5	0.07	54.97
NDX100	RSI2 < 1	Above 200-day MA	2 days	−0.17	6	8	75	0.14	54.62
NDX100	RSI2 < 1	Above 200-day MA	1 week	−0.86	3	8	37.5	0.36	57.34
NDX100	RSI2 < 2	Above 200-day MA	1 day	0.95	26	38	68.42	0.07	54.97
NDX100	RSI2 < 2	Above 200-day MA	2 days	0.97	26	38	68.42	0.14	54.62
NDX100	RSI2 < 2	Above 200-day MA	1 week	0.41	25	38	65.79	0.36	57.34
NDX100	RSI2 < 5	Above 200-day MA	1 day	0.41	90	145	62.07	0.07	54.97
NDX100	RSI2 < 5	Above 200-day MA	2 days	0.56	91	145	62.76	0.14	54.62
NDX100	RSI2 < 5	Above 200-day MA	1 week	0.67	93	145	64.14	0.36	57.34
NDX100	RSI2 > 99	Below 200-day MA	1 day	0.18	8	11	72.73	0.04	52.52
NDX100	RSI2 > 99	Below 200-day MA	2 days	1.01	8	11	72.73	0.06	50.85
NDX100	RSI2 > 99	Below 200-day MA	1 week	2.23	9	11	81.82	0.14	53.26
NDX100	RSI2 > 98	Below 200-day MA	1 day	−0.46	12	23	52.17	0.04	52.52
NDX100	RSI2 > 98	Below 200-day MA	2 days	−0.84	11	23	47.83	0.06	50.85
NDX100	RSI2 > 98	Below 200-day MA	1 week	−0.36	13	23	56.52	0.14	53.26
NDX100	RSI2 > 95	Below 200-day MA	1 day	−0.27	40	77	51.95	0.04	52.52

NDX100	RSI2 > 95	Below 200-day MA	2 days	−0.57	35	77	45.45	0.06	50.85
NDX100	RSI2 > 95	Below 200-day MA	1 week	−0.28	35	77	45.45	0.14	53.26
NDX100	RSI2 < 1	Below 200-day MA	1 day	0.53	24	43	55.81	0.04	52.52
NDX100	RSI2 < 1	Below 200-day MA	2 days	1.48	30	43	69.77	0.06	50.85
NDX100	RSI2 < 1	Below 200-day MA	1 week	1.64	28	43	65.12	0.14	53.26
NDX100	RSI2 < 2	Below 200-day MA	1 day	0.39	36	72	50	0.04	52.52
NDX100	RSI2 < 2	Below 200-day MA	2 days	1.13	44	72	61.11	0.06	50.85
NDX100	RSI2 < 2	Below 200-day MA	1 week	1.45	44	72	61.11	0.14	53.26
NDX100	RSI2 < 5	Below 200-day MA	1 day	0.61	88	162	54.32	0.04	52.52
NDX100	RSI2 < 5	Below 200-day MA	2 days	0.9	97	162	59.88	0.06	50.85
NDX100	RSI2 < 5	Below 200-day MA	1 week	1.51	106	162	65.43	0.14	53.26

Conclusion and Summary

Even though we do not suggest using only one indicator, if one had to, the 2-period RSI would be the indicator. Having researched and published our findings extensively since 2003, time has shown that it's the single best quantified indicator available for traders.

CHAPTER 12

Historical Volatility

We'd like to use this chapter to focus on individual stocks over a one-year period of time.

We're going to show how historical volatility (HV) has had a predictive ability in stocks. What you will see is that high volatility stocks (often momentum stocks) may look very exciting along the way, but over the next 252 trading days (one year) they have significantly underperformed the overall market. What you will also see is that low-volatility stocks, usually established large cap companies, have provided better returns and better stability for portfolios.

Historical volatility is the realized volatility of a financial instrument over a given time period. Generally, this measure is calculated by determining the average deviation from the average price of a financial instrument in the given time period. Standard deviation is the most common way to calculate historical volatility. Stocks with a higher historical volatility usually require a higher risk tolerance because they are obviously more volatile.

Here is how we ran our test:

1. We looked at all stocks above $5 per share whose average daily volume was at least 250,000 shares for the past one trading month. This includes all delisted stocks (meaning Enron, Lehman, buyouts, etc. were included in the test).
2. We separated the entire stock universe equally into five equal buckets ranked by their 100-day HV. The 20 percent of the stocks with the lowest 100-day HV were placed in bucket one. The next lowest were placed in bucket two, all the way through to the 20 percent with the highest 100-day HV which went into bucket five.
3. We did not cherry pick calendar days (meaning we looked only at the one-year calendar returns). We looked at every 252 trading days return (approximately one year), for every stock, since 1995. This means our test results encompassed over 4,000 one-year time frames. The reason we did this is because in reality, people don't invest only on the first day of the year. New money comes into the market every day, and this is the truest and best way to properly test a market strategy.

Let's now look at the test results.

TABLE 12.1 Historical Volatility (100-day) Test Results, 1/1/1995 to 9/30/2011 (8,058 symbols)

	Bucket	Return 252 Trading Days	% Winners	Avg % Loss of Losing Trades
Lowest HV	1	9.7%	66.0%	−19.8%
	2	10.3%	61.1%	−25.2%
	3	10.6%	56.7%	−30.9%
	4	9.8%	51.1%	−37.4%
Highest HV	5	5.4%	44.2%	−44.4%

Here are the highlights of the results:

1. First and most obvious, avoid the high flyers—meaning the stocks with the highest volatility. In many cases these are go-go story stocks. Yes, their charts look very pretty on the way up. They also tend to devastate portfolio returns on the way down (as an example look at JDSU in 2008 and NFLX in the 2011).
   Whereas the lowest HV stocks lost money only 34 percent of the full time, with an average loss of 19.8 percent, over 55 percent of the stocks with the highest HV lost money with the losers losing on average 44.4 percent per trade. Thank you, but no thank you.
2. A portfolio manager simply avoiding the stocks in the highest bucket (meaning the one with the highest volatility) and passively holding the remaining stocks on an unweighted basis would have greatly outperformed the market indices since 1995.
3. Lower volatility stocks provide greater stability in a portfolio. They have provided steady upside with increased lower volatility and lower risk.

Conclusion and Summary

It's been thought for many decades that one needs to be in riskier stocks in order to achieve greater returns. This test empirically shows the opposite to be true. We originally published this research in 2007, and we've seen on a go-forward basis how well this has held up, especially in 2008. The academic world has also published studies on the same concept, in many cases using beta to back this theory.

Look to invest in lower volatility stocks if you are a long-term investor. And in most cases, avoid the higher volatility stocks. If history is any guide, your portfolio will likely perform much better and be far safer if you do.

CHAPTER 13

Creating a Sample Strategy from This Research

By now you have a solid understanding of how markets have worked over the past two decades. What we'd like to do now is show you how to put together a very simple rotational system trading *S&P 500 stocks* using a few of the concepts you just learned.

This strategy you are about to learn has outperformed the S&P 500 index by on average over 10 percent a year, returning a cumulative net of triple-digit returns with 70 percent less volatility than the S&P 500 index.

Here are the rules; then we'll look at the test results, and we'll discuss why the simulated performance has performed so well over the past decade.

1. We took the S&P 500 index universe since January 1, 2001. All stocks traded in the index universe were included. Dividends, splits, buyouts, and so on were included in the test results.
2. The simulated trades were done once a week each Friday on the close.
3. For trades to be considered, the S&P must have been above its 200-day moving average on the trade date. We saw throughout the book that returns tend to be better when the S&P is above the 200-day moving average (when prices are trending higher).
4. In the spirit of rule three, only stocks above their 200-day moving average (MA) qualify for consideration. Therefore, both the S&P 500 index and the individual stock must be above the 200-day MA.
5. Using the multiple down days concept, we require the stock to be down two days in a row (yesterday and today).
6. Using the RSI concept, we require the stock to be oversold. In this case the RSI must be under 15 (going lower gives too few trades, though they tend to be better performing trades when they trigger).
7. Using the historical volatility concept we want the stock to have lower volatility. Therefore, we will only trade stocks whose 100-day historical volatility is below 35.
8. On the close on Friday buy up to 10 percent per position with up to 10 total positions. If more than 10 stocks qualify, take the ones that have the highest

100-day historical volatility (short term we want these stocks to have the ability to move).

9. Exit the next Friday on the close and rotate into the next round of 10 S&P 500 stocks.

This is a very simple rotational strategy to identify longer-term up trending S&P 500 stocks that have pulled back in a longer-term up trending market.

Here are the test results using one cent per share commissions to buy and one cent per share to sell.

TABLE 13.1 Monthly, Annual, and Total Returns from 1/1/2001 through 9/30/2011 for the S&P 500 Sample Strategy

	Jan	Feb	Mar	Apr	May	Jun	Jul	Aug	Sep	Oct	Nov	Dec	Annual Return	SP500	Difference
2001	0.41%	0.38%	0.37%	0.33%	0.31%	0.28%	0.31%	0.29%	0.20%	0.20%	0.16%	0.14%	3.42%	−13.04%	16.46%
2002	−1.35%	0.13%	−0.58%	−0.21%	0.15%	0.13%	0.15%	0.13%	0.14%	0.14%	0.10%	0.11%	−0.97%	−23.37%	22.40%
2003	0.10%	0.09%	0.11%	3.90%	3.49%	0.78%	−0.69%	3.13%	−4.67%	6.81%	4.33%	2.66%	21.41%	26.38%	−4.98%
2004	1.16%	2.42%	0.61%	−0.34%	2.99%	5.58%	−6.56%	0.13%	−1.27%	0.94%	1.50%	5.16%	12.42%	8.99%	3.43%
2005	−0.14%	2.52%	2.57%	−6.19%	1.39%	3.57%	10.42%	−0.17%	3.25%	−2.62%	3.44%	0.96%	19.72%	3.00%	16.72%
2006	7.73%	−3.67%	4.13%	4.68%	−3.02%	−0.34%	−0.72%	2.18%	3.27%	4.29%	0.09%	0.29%	19.92%	13.62%	6.30%
2007	3.39%	1.59%	3.87%	8.29%	−0.28%	−0.79%	−2.50%	−4.49%	3.44%	1.66%	−2.04%	1.18%	13.44%	3.53%	9.91%
2008	0.24%	0.17%	0.11%	0.11%	0.14%	0.16%	0.14%	0.14%	0.10%	0.06%	0.01%	0.00%	1.39%	−38.49%	39.87%
2009	0.01%	0.02%	0.02%	0.01%	0.01%	0.50%	−0.80%	3.52%	5.18%	−3.04%	5.54%	2.99%	14.50%	23.45%	−8.95%
2010	−3.24%	3.60%	9.16%	3.87%	−6.59%	−0.88%	0.01%	−3.51%	0.98%	5.12%	1.74%	1.91%	11.78%	12.78%	−1.00%
2011	3.98%	4.74%	2.78%	2.05%	−1.65%	0.31%	−1.10%	−11.31%	0.00%				−1.14%	−10.04%	8.90%
	10.48%	CAGR			−14.98%	Max DD Daily			0.81	Sharpe Ratio			0.41	Correlation to SP500	
	0.04%	CAGR SP500			−55.25%	Max DD Daily SP500			−0.03	Sharpe Ratio SP500					

161

This very simple method has shown a cumulative return of well over 100 percent while the S&P 500 index itself has been barely profitable during this period of time. There were only two small down years (2011 results are for nine months yet they still substantially beat the S&P 500 index). The method also saw consistency with no one year out of the ordinary. Also because of the 200-day rule on the S&P and on the stocks, 2008 was a positive performing year, not only substantially outperforming the averages but allowing investors to protect themselves from a major bear market.

What are the shortcomings of this portfolio (and just know every portfolio ever created has shortcomings)? The first is that fills are tough to come by on Friday's close especially if one is trading in size in a fund. Therefore, the slippage could be high, which would lower the returns. Fortunately we have been able to overcome this and create a large number of rotational strategies by placing in a few additional rules and then testing the results buying and selling on the average price of the day. This can then be traded on all days of the week (not just Friday), holding the positions one week (e.g., Tuesday–Tuesday, Wednesday–Wednesday, etc.).

If you would like more information on how to do this in a basket of S&P 500 stocks, they are programmed in our software product *The Machine*, and also in the software product for RIAs, *The Machine Advisor*. More information can be obtained by calling 973-494-7311 ext. 1 or online at www.TheMachineUS.com.

Conclusion and Summary

We felt it was important to add a portfolio strategy to the second edition of the book. It allows you to see how by taking a few ideas from the book, you can potentially improve your returns in a low-risk manner. These are concepts backed by over two decades of quantified market behavior, and there is an abundance of ways to use this information to help you successfully manage and grow your money.

CHAPTER 14

Applying the Information in This Book

By now we suspect you realize that a lot of the information found in this book flies in the face conventional wisdom. In Chapter 1 we discussed how Bill James' findings, chronicled by Michael Lewis in *Moneyball*, and now successfully used by a number of baseball teams, defied decades of thinking in the baseball world. The findings in this book do the same for the financial world. Just as old-school baseball attempted to use the imprecise art of gut and intuition to make decisions, Wall Street and the media do the same when it comes to interpreting markets. Decades of lore, repeated over and over again have become fact, without a shred of quantitative evidence. And, as we have seen from the behavior of the market over the past two decades, *much of what is thought to be true is simply wrong*. The statistics prove this out.

There is a wealth of information in this book. And there are many ways you can use this information. One theme that is very, very obvious is that there has been one consistent way that the market has worked over the past 22 years. *It is that buying market weakness has been superior to buying strength. And it also is very apparent that selling into strength has been better than selling into weakness.* We came to these conclusions after we looked at the market using some of the most popular indicators.

These conclusions were confirmed in many different ways, by comparing multiple-days' highs to multiple-days' lows; comparing multiple days of the market rising to multiple days of the market declining; comparing multiple days of the market rising higher intraday to declining lower intraday; looking at the days when the market rose strongly to the days it declined sharply; studying days when advancing issues were much stronger than declining issues; looking at the put/call ratio, the two-period Relative Strength Index (RSI), and studying the effects of prices when the volatility index is stretched to extremes. The test results, many using over 5,500 days of trading, all point us in the same direction—*it remains smarter, wiser, and more profitable* to be buying weakness and selling strength in stocks, than vice versa.

There are no assurances that any of these findings will hold up in the future. There is no guarantee of the market ever acting in any one manner. But, if the past history continues to hold, there are edges here for you to consider in your trading and your investing.

How can you use these results? One could probably write multiple books on this, but we'll provide you with some direction.

1. Should you decide to apply this research to your trading, *you should not use any of these indicators blindly*. No matter how big the edge has been during some of these times, there have also been large drawdowns in many along the way. Prudent money management and portfolio management (risk control and position size) is a must. In fact, they may be as important if not more important as any trading strategy.

2. We used static time frames for the exit (this means in most cases we used one-day, two-day, and one-week exits). *The results can be improved by using dynamic exits such as price movement or with additional indicators.* For example, waiting for prices to close on the other side of their 5-period moving average. The test results often improve dramatically by using this dynamic exit as opposed to a static exit. Again, this is something we encourage you to pursue further.

3. If you believe that markets move from overbought to oversold and oversold to over-bought, you will want to structure your entire thought process around this. This means looking to be buying the times when the market has had a statistical edge to the long side and looking to exit when the edge is exhausted. This is especially true in bull markets, meaning markets that are trading above their 200-day moving average. And, if you short stocks, you should be looking to be a seller when the market has shown strength, especially when it's trading below its 200-day moving average. As you have seen, historically this has been where some of the biggest edges have existed.

4. Having multiple signals indicating the same thing will improve the performance of many of the indicators. We gave you the results of these indicators as they stood alone. We encourage you to use them in combination.

5. Based on the results in this book (along with our own observations) we personally will likely never buy short-term strength again, nor sell short into short-term weakness. And, if we have our way, our kids and their kids never will, either. To us, the statistics are too strong to do otherwise.

6. What about fundamental analysis? Good question. We were only looking at the validity of common entry techniques and indicators. Fundamentals may improve results, but what has always been interesting to us is the fact that fundamentals are probably one of the easiest areas to test, as the information is vast. Yet in spite of the fact that Wall Street research (both from the brokerage firms and the independent research firms) is overwhelmingly fundamentally driven, there still remains today **little quantified evidence** that **their research actually has a statistical edge**.

7. Our research focused only on looking at the market over the very short-term. Successful short-term trading is made up of taking advantage of small edges and executing properly from there. It's very difficult to make money trading if you're buying into periods that have historically produced negative returns.

8. We've touched upon this fact throughout the book, and we need to touch on it again. *Don't get caught up in the hype, especially the hype that the media creates, when the market is very strong or when it's very weak.* The press has a habit after a few down days of quoting analysts who pronounce that "the market is breaking

down," "things look bad," "the breadth is terrible," and so forth. And after the market has had a number of strong up-days, just the opposite happens: They're jumping up and down with excitement.

Markets absolutely do not move in one direction neither short-term, nor long-term. They move from overbought to oversold and vice versa (this has been shown over and over again throughout this book). Yes, there has been a 100-year upward long-term bias, but it's filled with times the market has sold off and sometimes sold off sharply. You only have to look back at years like 2000–2002 and 2008 to know this. If strength was always followed by strength the market would be at infinity, not at the 11,800-level as of this writing. And if weakness always followed through, we would be at zero. Sorry, not only is the concept that strong markets always lead to strong markets illogical, this book statistically proves it is illogical. The media and the analysts most times have it wrong, especially at extremes.

Once again, the stock market moves from overbought to oversold and vice versa, over and over again. The statistics prove this out. It's happened in one way or another for the past 100 years and in our opinion, it will happen for the next 100 years. The key from here is to properly identify when the market really is overbought and when it really is oversold. We hope this book now provides you with a strong statistical perspective of "How Markets Really Work."

About the Authors

Larry Connors has more than 30 years of experience working in the financial markets industry. He is managing partner of LCA Capital, an asset management firm, and Connors Research, a financial markets research company. He has built two multimillion-dollar financial market companies since 1995 including The Connors Group, a financial markets information company. In 2009, The Connors Group was twice chosen as one of the 10 fastest-growing private companies by the Entrex Private Company Index.

Larry started his career in 1982 at Merrill Lynch and later moved on to become a vice president with Donaldson, Lufkin, Jenrette (DLJ). He has authored top-selling books on market strategies and volatility trading, including *How Markets Really Work*, *Street Smarts* (with Linda Raschke), and *High Probability ETF Trading*. His books have been translated into German, Italian, Spanish, Russian, Japanese, and Chinese.

Larry's opinions and insights have been featured and quoted in the *Wall Street Journal*, *New York Times*, *Barron's*, Bloomberg TV & Radio, *Bloomberg Magazine*, Dow Jones Newswire, Yahoo! Finance, E-Trade Financial Daily, and many others. He has also been a featured speaker at a number of major investment conferences over the past two decades.

Larry is also the creator of The Machine and, most recently, The Machine Advisor. The Machine Advisor is web-based investment decision support software that allows financial advisors to differentiate their practice through both innovative active investing strategies and interactive sales and marketing tools.

Cesar Alvarez is the director of research for Connors Research.

Cesar was a senior designer of Excel in the 1990s, helping Microsoft further create and build out Excel. For the past nine years Cesar has been a professional investor and researcher.

Cesar has been at the forefront of stock market research, having developed a number of successful trading systems now used by numerous investors and fund managers in the United States and internationally. Cesar holds a Bachelors of Science in Electrical Engineering and Computer Science and a Masters of Science in Computer Science from the University of California, Berkeley.

Index